→ Maths revision to the power of ten

MATHS *Virgin*

GCSE PASS

GCSE PASS

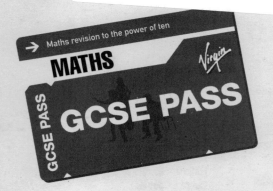

Daphne Perridge

VIRGIN REVISION GUIDE POWERED BY *Letts*

Contents

Section 4 Handling Data

Virgin Help Section

Welcome to *Virgin GCSE Maths Revision Guide*. This unique pocket guide is designed to help your revision and boost your knowledge as you prepare for your GCSEs.

A team of revision experts has created this book to help you save time, avoid exam stress and make sure you get the **best possible result**. Here's how it works ...

Exam survival

Our expert advice on how to survive your exams will get you started; help you plan an effective revision programme; give you top tips on how to remember the key information; test your progress and reveal how best to survive the actual exams.

All you need to know

The information in this book is based on the core topics within the **Key Stage 4 National Curriculum** and **all GCSE exam specifications**. However, unlike textbooks or other revision guides, it covers the essential information in **just the right level of detail**.

The book is divided into four clear sections: Number; Algebra; Shape, Space and Measures and Handling Data. Each section contains all the specific topics you need to know to guarantee GCSE success.

Learn fast

Because each topic is presented on a single page, you can zoom in on the really essential information straight away. Start with the **Key Fact** at the top of the page, get to grips with the detail underneath and make sure you check out the **Grade Booster** comment before you test your knowledge on the opposite page.

Testing time

You've just read it, but do you know it? Well here's how to find out. Use the **Question Bank** to see if you really know your stuff. Check the answer section in the back of the book and if you got all the questions right, move on. If not, read the information again to see if you missed anything, then try again. Remember to revisit the Question Banks from time to time to make sure that the information has really sunk in.

Keeping your score

At the back of the book you will find a **Scoring Grid** where you can keep tabs on your progress. Keep your scores as you work through the book and see if you can spot any patterns emerging. For example, did you get more correct answers in the Number and Handling Data sections? Then maybe you need to focus your learning on the Algebra or Shape, Space and Measures sections. **Remember, these are your results – use them to get even better!**

And there's more

Want to find out more? Well help is at hand. We have included a **glossary** of key mathematical words and easy-to-understand definitions plus a list of useful **websites** that will help improve your knowledge and understanding.

Don't know where to start? Can't remember the key information? Worried about sitting the exam? Read on and get your questions answered.

You already know more than you think

The fact is that you've probably already encountered the key information you need for success at GCSE. Over a two-year period, you'll have been taught all of the core topics on your GCSE specification and your teachers will have explained the course structure and how it's examined. You'll have done a fair few homeworks, tests and, no doubt, some form of coursework. All of this counts and shouldn't be underestimated. All you need to do in the run-up to your GCSE exams is to **revisit the information**, bring it to the **forefront of your mind** and **programme it into your memory**.

Make a plan

Use your class notes and put them into a logical order. You'll soon build up an idea of the topics you have to revise and whether you're missing any key areas. If you're still unsure about certain areas of the course, check the relevant sections in this book or ask your teachers – that's what they're there for!

Work out the time you have available before the exams and exactly what needs to be revised. **Be realistic** – don't kid yourself that you'll do 8 hours of revision every day for 3 months. You have to eat, sleep, exercise and have a life too! It may be a relief to know that short bursts of revision, say about 30 minutes at a time, followed by a break are the most effective. A **manageable plan** covering all topics and setting a realistic number of hours for revision each week is the way forward.

From time to time go back and **revisit topics** that you have already revised. This will help you check your progress and also it will lock the information in your **long-term memory**.

Finally, it may sound obvious but don't forget the importance of **noting the dates of all your exams**. This will affect what you revise and when, not to mention making sure that you turn up on the right days!

Top revision techniques

There are several proven revision techniques to help you remember information more easily. None of these memory-boosting techniques are difficult to grasp, but everyone is different and some may work better for you than others. Try them all and find the method that suits you best.

For most students this means making your revision as **ACTIVE** as possible. For example, simply reading pages and pages may not make the information sink in. Why not use the same system that we have used in this book: read a page of information, write some questions, have a short break and then test yourself?

In the same way, try some of these techniques to trigger your memory whilst revising:

- Try condensing your notes into short, **revision cards**. You will learn as you go and you will build up a great library of Key Fact cards. Choose key words rather than write full sentences. Break up the text with bullet points or numbers. Use a highlighter pen or underlining to emphasise the most important words.

- Using **different colours** will help the brain store and recall information. Try writing in up to four different colours, but try to be consistent and, for example, always use blue for '*causes*' and red for '*effects*'.

- **Be visual** – use drawings and labelled diagrams. A well-labelled diagram is an excellent way of recording information on a revision card. Diagrams should be kept very simple so they can be memorised and reproduced during the exam.

- **Idea maps, flow charts** and **spider diagrams**. Simple flow charts and idea maps link information together, especially where there is a process or sequence of events. A few words in boxes joined by arrows are all that is required. For example, a simple process may be shown as '*insert cash card → key in PIN → select service required → key in amount → press Accept → take card → take money*'.

- Drawing **humorous cartoons** makes revising more fun, and information easier to recall. To remember that 'Bearings are measured clockwise from the North line', draw a North line with a clock (and a polar bear too, if you like) beside it.

- Make up **rhymes** and **mnemonics** to remember key facts. This is a very powerful way of learning and recalling information. A simple mnemonic technique uses the first letters of words to recall lists, for example,
  Trig ratios = **S**ir **O**liver's **H**orse **C**ame **A**mbling **H**ome **T**o **O**liver's **A**unt
  (**S**in = **o**pposite/**h**ypotenuse, **c**os = **a**djacent/**h**ypotenuse, **t**an = **o**pposite/**a**djacent).

- **Repeat facts** out loud or why not try recording them onto a tape? You can then listen to them in different situations, e.g. waiting for a bus, doing the washing up, on the toilet!

- Try **testing** a classmate, a parent or a friend. We all love a quiz and asking questions is a great way of boosting your memory.

The more your revision involves you *doing* something rather than simply reading, and the more visual it is, the more information you will find you retain.

- ***Test yourself***

  It may sound corny, but 'practice really does make perfect'. As soon as you feel confident enough, you should attempt some practice questions. Try to familiarise yourself with the style of exam questions by highlighting the key words in the question. Get into the habit of planning your response before you actually start writing and then checking that your answer stays relevant as you write.

  The thing *not* to do with practice questions is to attempt them before you have revised. Learn your stuff *first* and then test yourself. You will soon see the progress you have made or be able to identify any areas that you find particularly difficult.

The big day

If you've worked hard studying and revising in the run-up to your GCSEs, do yourself one last favour and make sure you **don't panic** in the exam.

Very few people enjoy sitting exams, however everyone can make the experience less stressful by remembering the following exam techniques.

- **Read the instructions on the exam paper.** This is obvious, but really, really important. Take particular notice of the time allowed for the exam and the number of questions you are asked to attempt. Make sure you do this for every subject and every paper.

- **Pace yourself** through the exam. Read each question carefully and underline the key words to help focus and plan your answers. Remember to check the marks available for each question and to allocate your time accordingly.

- **Stay calm** no matter what the paper throws at you. Whilst it is advisable to attempt every question, you can always leave a difficult question until the end and come back to it once you have finished the rest of the paper. Even if you think you can only do the first part it's worth starting a question. Inspiration often comes as you get into it.

- Finally, leave some time to **check through your answers**. Don't be tempted to cross out and change lots of answers in the last five minutes of the exam, rather use this time to check that your writing is legible, your spelling is accurate, you've given answers to the number of decimal points (d.p.) or significant figures (s.f.) asked for and that you've done the best you can.

Good luck!

We hope you find this book useful – and enjoy using it. GCSE exams are important and can be stressful, but if you prepare properly and do your best, you will succeed. Remember, once the exams are over ... well, we'll leave all that to you!

SECTION 1 NUMBER

Integers

This is a straightforward topic. 'Integer' just means whole number and integers can be positive (+) or negative (–) with 0 (zero) in between.

A number line is a good way to show integers.

integers getting smaller · integers getting bigger

−6 −5 −4 −3 −2 −1 0 1 2 3 4 5 6

You can add, subtract, multiply and divide integers.

Take care when working with negative integers.

■ When you add a positive and a negative integer, the positive and negative parts cancel each other out as far as possible.

$$5 + (-6) = -1 \qquad\qquad -3 + 7 = 4$$

■ When you multiply or divide a positive integer by a negative integer (or vice versa), the answer is negative.

$$12 \div (-4) = -3 \qquad\qquad -8 \times 2 = -16$$
$$-9 \div 3 = -3 \qquad\qquad 7 \times (-5) = -35$$

■ When you multiply or divide a negative integer by a negative integer, the answer is positive.

$$-36 \div (-9) = 4 \qquad\qquad -8 \times (-5) = 40$$

Question Bank 1

1 Work out: $10 + 4 - 6$

2 $(-7) + (-4) - (-8)$ is:

   a -19 ☐   b 19 ☐

   c -3 ☐   d 5 ☐

3 True or false?

   -5 is less than -6.

4 What is $30 \div (-3)$?

5 Choose the correct answer.

   -30 is equal to:

   (i) 5×6 (iii) $5 \times (-6)$

   (ii) $(-5) \times 6$ (iv) $(-5) \times (-6)$

   a (i) and (ii) only ☐   b (ii) and (iii) only ☐

   c (iii) and (iv) only ☐ d (i) and (iv) only ☐

6 Write these integers in order, smallest first.

   $-3, 11, -7, 0, 2, 5$

GRADE BOOSTER

Learn the rules for combining positive and negative integers.

plus × plus = plus	**plus ÷ plus = plus**
plus × minus = minus	**plus ÷ minus = minus**
minus × plus = minus	**minus ÷ plus = minus**
minus × minus = plus	**minus ÷ minus = plus**

Factors and multiples

Factors go into a number exactly. You get multiples by writing out the multiplication table for a number.

■ 2 is a **factor** of 24 because it divides exactly into 24.

$24 \div 2 = 12$

The factors of 24 are 1, 2, 3, 4, 6, 8, 12, 24.

■ **Multiples** of 5 are $1 \times 5, 2 \times 5, 3 \times 5, 4 \times 5, \ldots$ i.e. 5, 10, 15, 20, ...

Some numbers have only two factors: 1 and themselves. They are called **prime numbers.** The prime numbers between 1 and 20 are:

2, 3, 5, 7, 11, 13, 17, 19

■ You can write any integer as a product of prime factors.

$10 = 2 \times 5 \qquad 12 = 2 \times 2 \times 3$

■ Some numbers have common factors, e.g.

factors of 12 = **1, 2, 3**, 4, **6**, 12

factors of 18 = **1, 2, 3, 6**, 9, 18

The common factors of 12 and 18 are 1, 2, 3 and 6.

The **highest common factor (HCF)** of 12 and 18 is 6.

■ Two (or more) numbers have common multiples, e.g.

multiples of 4 = 4, 8, 12, 16, 20, 24, **28**, 32, ...

multiples of 7 = 7, 14, 21, **28**, 35, ...

The **lowest common multiple (LCM)** of 4 and 7 is 28.

Question Bank 2

1 Fill in the gaps.

  Factors of 36 = __, __, 3, __, 6, 9, __, __, 36

2 6 is a _____ of 24.

3 List the first five multiples of 9.

4 Find the HCF of 36 and 60.

5 How many prime numbers are there between 80 and 100?

6 The LCM of 12 and 18 is:

  a 6   ☐

  b 12   ☐

  c 72   ☐

  d 36   ☐

7 Write 48 as a product of prime factors.

GRADE BOOSTER
1 is not a prime number (it does not have two factors). Knowing this impresses the examiner!

Decimals 1

Here are the basics for understanding decimals. In a decimal, the decimal point separates the whole number part from the fractions. The fractions are tenths, hundredths, thousandths and so on, e.g.

$$35.742 = 35 + \frac{7}{10} + \frac{4}{100} + \frac{2}{1000} \text{ or } 35 + \frac{742}{1000}$$

- The value of each digit in the number depends on its place.

  What is the value of the 2 in each of these numbers: 27.906, 0.042, 3.2?

    In 27.906 the 2 is worth $2 \times 10 = 20$

    In 0.042 the 2 is worth $2 \times \frac{1}{1000} = \frac{2}{1000}$

    In 3.27 the 2 is worth $2 \times \frac{1}{10} = \frac{2}{10}$

- To change a fraction into a decimal, divide the numerator (top number) by the denominator (bottom number).

Write $\frac{3}{4}$ and $\frac{2}{5}$ as decimals.

$$4{\overline{)3.00}}^{0.75} \qquad \frac{3}{4} = 0.75 \qquad 5{\overline{)2.0}}^{0.4} \qquad \frac{2}{5} = 0.4$$

- 0.75 and 0.4 are called **terminating decimals**, because they stop!
- **Terminating** decimals can be written as fractions.

Here's how to write 0.137 and 0.8903 as fractions.

Look at the place value of the last decimal digit to find the denominator of the fraction.

In 0.137 the 7 is $\frac{7}{1000}$ so the denominator is 1000, so $0.137 = \frac{137}{1000}$

In 0.8903 the 3 is $\frac{3}{10\,000}$ so $0.8903 = \frac{8903}{10\,000}$

- Terminating decimals come from fractions with denominators whose factors

  are factors of 10, or 100, or 1000 etc., e.g. $\frac{1}{2}$, $\frac{1}{4}$, $\frac{1}{5}$, $\frac{1}{8}$, $\frac{1}{10}$.

Question Bank 3

1 What does the 3 in 56.7038 stand for?

   a 3 ☐   **b** $\frac{3}{10}$ ☐

   c $\frac{3}{100}$ ☐   **d** $\frac{3}{1000}$ ☐

2 Which is greater, 0.835 or 0.84?

3 Write $50 + 8 + \frac{6}{10} + \frac{5}{100}$ as a decimal number.

4 Write $\frac{7}{8}$ as a decimal.

5 Write 0.6 as a fraction.

6 Write 0.55 as a fraction in its lowest terms.

GRADE BOOSTER

Keep the decimal points in line under each other in calculations and the decimal places will take care of themselves.

Decimals 2

> Let's take a look at recurring decimals. $\frac{1}{3}$ is a recurring decimal. When
> you change $\frac{1}{3}$ to a decimal you divide 3 into 1.000 and you can carry
> on dividing forever.
>
> $$\frac{1}{3} = 3\overline{)1.000}^{\,0.333} = 0.\dot{3}$$ *The dot over the 3 shows that it recurs.*

■ **Recurring** decimals can be written as *exact* fractions.

Examples: Write $0.\dot{3}$ and $0.\dot{2}\dot{7}$ as fractions.

$$10 \times 0.333... = 3.333...$$ (1) (one recurring figure, so multiply by 10)

$$\underline{1 \times 0.333... = 0.333...}$$ (2) Subtract (2) from (1)

$$9 \times 0.333... = 3$$

$$0.333... = \frac{3}{9} = \frac{1}{3}$$

$$100 \times 0.2727... = 27.2727...$$ (1) (two recurring figures, so multiply by 100)

$$\underline{1 \times 0.2727... = 0.2727...}$$ (2) Subtract (2) from (1)

$$99 \times 0.2727... = 27$$

$$0.2727... = \frac{27}{99} = \frac{3}{11}$$

■ Recurring decimals come from fractions with denominators that have
factors that are not factors of 10, e.g. $\frac{1}{6}$, $\frac{1}{7}$, $\frac{1}{9}$, $\frac{1}{11}$.

This is what happens when you write $\frac{1}{7}$ as a decimal.

$$\frac{1}{7} = 7\overline{)1.000000000000}^{\,0.142857142857} = 0.\dot{1}4285\dot{7}$$

To turn this recurring decimal into a fraction you would have to multiply by
$1\,000\,000$, unless of course you recognised it as $\frac{1}{7}$!

Question Bank 4

1 Match each fraction with a decimal.

  a $\dfrac{1}{3}$　　　　**b** $\dfrac{33}{100}$　　　　**c** $\dfrac{3}{10}$

  (i) 0.33　　　**(ii)** 0.3　　　**(iii)** $0.\dot{3}$

2 Which of these fractions are terminating decimals?

  a $\dfrac{5}{6}$ ☐　　　　**b** $\dfrac{3}{8}$ ☐

  c $\dfrac{3}{4}$ ☐　　　　**d** $\dfrac{7}{10}$ ☐

  e $\dfrac{4}{7}$ ☐

3 Write $\dfrac{5}{12}$ as a decimal.

4 To change to a fraction, first multiply by

  a 10
  b 100 ☐
  c 1000 ☐
  d 0.1 ☐

5 Arrange in order of size, smallest first.

  $\dfrac{1}{4}$　　　0.27　　　$\dfrac{2}{9}$

GRADE BOOSTER

If you remember to write $\dfrac{1}{3}$ and $\dfrac{2}{3}$ as $0.\dot{3}$ and $0.\dot{6}$ the examiner will be impressed.

17

Fractions 1

> A fraction is part of a whole. In the fraction $\frac{3}{4}$, the top number, 3, is the **numerator**.
>
> The bottom number, 4, is the **denominator**.

- $\frac{3}{4}, \frac{6}{8}, \frac{9}{12}$ are **equivalent fractions**.

$$\frac{3}{4} \qquad \frac{6}{8} \qquad \frac{9}{12}$$

To find three fractions equivalent to $\frac{5}{10}$, multiply or divide the numerator and denominator by the same number.

$$\frac{5}{10} = \frac{1}{2} = \frac{15}{30} \text{ (divide by 5 or multiply by 3)}$$

- To simplify fractions find the common factor of the numerator and the denominator and cancel.

a $\frac{25}{30} = \frac{5}{6}$ **b** $\frac{12}{15} = \frac{4}{5}$ **c** $\frac{4}{10} = \frac{2}{5}$

- Write these fractions in order, smallest first: $\frac{2}{3}, \frac{3}{5}, \frac{5}{8}$.

  Find a common denominator. $3 \times 5 \times 8 = 120$

  Find the equivalent fractions.

$$\frac{2}{3} = \frac{2 \times 5 \times 8}{120} = \frac{80}{120} \qquad \frac{3}{5} = \frac{3 \times 3 \times 8}{120} = \frac{72}{120} \qquad \frac{5}{8} = \frac{5 \times 3 \times 5}{120} = \frac{75}{120}$$

The order is $\frac{3}{5}, \frac{5}{8}, \frac{2}{3}$.

- Find two fractions between $\frac{1}{5}$ and $\frac{1}{3}$. $\frac{1}{5} = \frac{3}{15} = \frac{6}{30}$ $\frac{1}{3} = \frac{5}{15} = \frac{10}{30}$

So $\frac{7}{30}, \frac{8}{30}$ and $\frac{9}{30}$ are between $\frac{1}{5}$ and $\frac{1}{3}$. Choose any two.

Two fractions between $\frac{1}{5}$ and $\frac{1}{3}$ are $\frac{7}{30}$ and $\frac{8}{30}$.

Question Bank 5

1 What fraction is shaded?

2 Write down the equivalent fractions shown in the diagrams.

3 Fill in the missing numbers.

   a $\dfrac{5}{8} = \dfrac{}{32}$

   b $\dfrac{18}{} = \dfrac{3}{4}$

   c $\dfrac{11}{12} = \dfrac{33}{}$

4 Which fraction is equivalent to $\dfrac{4}{9}$?

   a $\dfrac{12}{27}$ ☐   **b** $\dfrac{3}{8}$ ☐   **c** $\dfrac{16}{45}$ ☐   **d** $\dfrac{5}{10}$ ☐

5 Find two fractions between $\dfrac{1}{5}$ and $\dfrac{1}{4}$.

6 Put these fractions in order, smallest first: $\dfrac{7}{15}$, $\dfrac{1}{2}$, $\dfrac{4}{9}$.

GRADE BOOSTER

'Simplify' and 'write in its lowest terms' mean cancel down the
fraction until there are no more common factors.

Fractions 2

> *Take fractions a bit at a time. When you feel confident with one part move on to the next.*

■ $2\frac{3}{4}$ is a **mixed number**. 2 whole ones is 8 quarters,

so $2\frac{3}{4} = 8 + 3$ quarters = 11 quarters. $2\frac{3}{4} = \frac{11}{4}$

■ $\frac{11}{4}$ is an **improper fraction.**

Change $5\frac{3}{8}$ to an improper fraction.

$5\frac{3}{8} = \left(5 \times \frac{8}{8}\right) + \frac{3}{8} = \frac{40}{8} + \frac{3}{8} = \frac{43}{8}$ (change the 5 to eighths, then add the $\frac{3}{8}$)

Change $\frac{16}{3}$ to a mixed number.

$16 \div 3 = 5$ r 1 so $\frac{16}{3} = 5\frac{1}{3}$ (divide the numerator, 16, by the denominator, 5)

■ Fractions can only be added and subtracted if their denominators are the same.

a $\frac{2}{3} + \frac{5}{6}$ The common denominator is 6. $\frac{2}{3} = \frac{4}{6}$, $\frac{4}{6} + \frac{5}{6} = \frac{9}{6} = 1\frac{3}{6} = 1\frac{1}{2}$

b $1\frac{3}{4} + 3\frac{7}{10} = 4\frac{15+14}{20} = 4\frac{29}{20} = 5\frac{9}{20}$

c $6\frac{5}{8} - 3\frac{1}{2} = 3\frac{5}{8} - \frac{1}{2}$ (subtract the whole numbers first)

$= 3\frac{5-4}{8} = 3\frac{1}{8}$

d $4\frac{1}{2} - 2\frac{7}{8} = 2\frac{1}{2} - \frac{7}{8}$ (subtract the whole numbers)

$= 2\frac{4}{8} - \frac{7}{8} = 1\frac{12}{8} - \frac{7}{8}$ (change 1 whole into eighths) $= 1\frac{5}{8}$

Question Bank 6

1 $3\frac{3}{8}$ is equal to:

   a $\frac{33}{8}$ ☐

   b $\frac{24}{8}$ ☐

   c $\frac{17}{8}$ ☐

   d $\frac{27}{8}$ ☐

2 Write $\frac{21}{5}$ as a mixed number.

3 Find $2\frac{5}{8} + 4\frac{1}{4}$.

4 $7\frac{1}{2} - 5\frac{3}{4}$ is:

   a $1\frac{3}{4}$ ☐   **c** $2\frac{1}{8}$ ☐

   b $2\frac{1}{4}$ ☐   **d** $1\frac{1}{4}$ ☐

5 Work out $2\frac{1}{2} + 3\frac{1}{3} - 1\frac{5}{12}$.

GRADE BOOSTER

Practise doing lots of additions and subtractions until you're confident.

Fractions 3

> *Take heart! Multiplying and dividing fractions is easier than adding and subtracting fractions. You don't have to find common denominators.*

■ To multiply two fractions, multiply the numerators and multiply the denominators.

Example $\frac{2}{3} \times \frac{5}{8} = \frac{10}{24} = \frac{5}{12}$ (Remember to simplify your answer.)

■ To divide by a fraction, turn the fraction upside down and multiply (that is, multiply by the reciprocal).

Example $\frac{7}{10} \div \frac{3}{4} = \frac{7}{10} \times \frac{4}{3} = \frac{28}{30} = \frac{14}{15}$

Using fractions

■ Now you know how to work with fractions you can use them in problems. This really convinces the examiner you're on top of things!

Example 1   Tom planted 48 daffodils. On Easter Day $\frac{2}{3}$ of them were flowering. How many was that?

$$\frac{2}{3} \times 48 = \frac{2 \times 48}{3} = \frac{96}{3} = 32$$

(To find a fraction of an amount multiply by the fraction.)

Example 2   Ed has £90. He spends £16 on CDs and £6.50 in a burger bar. What fraction of the original amount has he spent?

$16 + 6.50 = 22.50$ (total amount spent)

Fraction spent $= \frac{22.5}{90} = \frac{45}{180} = \frac{1}{4}$ (amount spent ÷ original amount)

Ed has spent $\frac{1}{4}$ of the original amount.

Question Bank 7

1 Half of $35\frac{1}{2}$ is:

   a $17\frac{1}{4}$ ☐   **c** $17\frac{1}{2}$ ☐

   b $17\frac{3}{4}$ ☐   **d** $17\frac{5}{8}$ ☐

2 Which is smaller, $\frac{3}{8}$ of £60 or $\frac{1}{3}$ of £70?

3 Rika pays $\frac{2}{5}$ of her income in tax and $\frac{1}{3}$ on living expenses. What fraction is left?

4 True or false? Half of a third of a quarter is the same as a quarter of a third of a half?

5 Ben can iron a shirt in $5\frac{3}{4}$ minutes. How many shirts can he iron in 46 minutes?

6 In a race, Billy Boy was $1\frac{1}{2}$ lengths ahead of Sunny Jim, and Sunny Jim was $\frac{2}{3}$ length ahead of Mumbo Jumbo. How far ahead of Mumbo Jumbo was Billy Boy?

GRADE BOOSTER

Before you rush in, decide whether you need to add, subtract, multiply or divide the fractions.

Approximation 1

This is a really useful skill that you probably already use without realising it! Numbers are often rounded to make them easier to handle. For instance, the crowd at a football match is usually rounded to the nearest thousand; the population of a country may be given to the nearest million; and you give your age to the last completed year.

■ Round these numbers to the nearest hundred.

a   450 = 500 to the nearest hundred   (halfway or more – round up)

b   1309 = 1300 to the nearest hundred   (less than halfway, so round down)

c   2073 = 2100 to the nearest hundred

■ Decimals can be rounded.

Round to 2 decimal places (d.p.):

a   53.137 = 53.14 to 2 d.p.

b   0.6525 = 0.65 to 2 d.p.

c   8.098 = 8.10 to 2 d.p.   (The 0 at the end shows the number has been rounded to 2 d.p.)

■ Significant figures are used to round whole numbers and decimals.

Round to 3 significant figures (s.f.):

a   3564 = 3560 to 3 s.f.   (You must put in the 0 to keep the digits in their correct places.)

b   0.0052864 = 0.00529 to 3 s.f.   (The 0s at the beginning of the number are not significant figures.)

c   14.081 = 14.1 to 3 s.f.

Question Bank 8

1 Round to 2 significant figures.

   a 339.5

   b 0.00519

2 Round to the nearest thousand.

   a 1 234 567

   b 500 495

3 Choose the correct answer.

   Which of the following are correct?

   The number 0.05703 is equal to 0.057 when rounded to

   (i) 3 s.f.   (ii) 2 s.f.   (iii) 3 d.p.   (iv) the nearest thousandth.

   a all of them ☐

   b (i), (iii) and (iv) only ☐

   c (ii) and (iv) only ☐

   d (ii), (iii) and (iv) only ☐

4 Round the numbers in this report to a reasonable degree of accuracy.

   11 783 people attended a football match. Adults paid £12.75 and children, £8.30. The total gate money was £147 483.05.

5 Find a) the area, b) the perimeter of this rectangle correct to 1 d.p.

   6.4 cm

   2.6 cm

GRADE BOOSTER

This topic crops up all over the place so it's worth getting to grips with it.

25

Approximation 2

> *Your calculator often gives lots of decimal places, but your answer is not more accurate because you write them all down. If you only measure to the nearest millimetre, then your answer is only accurate to the nearest millimetre.*

Here's an example.

Toni runs 100m in 8.2 seconds. What is her average speed?

$$\text{average speed} = \frac{100}{8.2}$$

The calculator answer is 12.195122m/s, but it would be silly to give all these decimal places. Round the answer to a suitable degree of accuracy.

Toni's speed is 12.2m/s to 3 s.f. (significant figures).

- Give the answer to the same degree of accuracy as the figures in the question.
- You can round figures in a calculation to get an approximate answer. This helps you spot calculator errors.

Estimate the answers to these calculations.

a $647 \times 0.32 \approx 600 \times 0.3 = 180$

(Round the figures to 1 s.f. The rule is: 5 or higher, round up.)

b $\dfrac{0.27 \times 48.4}{6.8} \approx \dfrac{0.3 \times 50}{7} = \dfrac{15}{7} \approx 2$ (You may need to round twice to get your estimate.)

- When estimating quantities you need to round.

  Rudolph has 44 Christmas cards to post. Stamps are in books of 6. How many books does he need?

$$44 \div 6 = 7 \text{ r } 2$$

7 books will not be enough so round up.

Rudolph needs 8 books of stamps.

Question Bank 9

1 Estimate the cost of a wedding for 200 guests at £28.50 per head.

2 $\frac{11.78 \div 0.64}{4.55}$ is approximately equal to:

   a 0.4

   b 40

   c 4

   d 0.04

3 Roughly how many potatoes are there in a 3 kg bag if the average weight of a potato is 150g?

4 Rana needs 16 lengths of wallpaper to decorate a bedroom. She can cut 3 lengths from each roll.

   How many rolls should she buy?

5 Match each calculation with its answer.

   a 7.2×9.8 b $13.92 \div 5.8$ c $8.8 \div 9.9$

   (i) 0.889   (ii) 70.56   (iii) 2.4

GRADE BOOSTER

Don't round during the intermediate steps of a calculation. You lose accuracy.

Approximation 3

> This topic isn't difficult if you do one step at a time. All measurements are approximate. Their accuracy depends on the precision of the measuring instrument and how skilfully it's used.

Examples

1 If Simon weighs 62 kg to the nearest kg, his weight can be anything between 61.5 kg and 62.5 kg (0.5 kg more or less than the stated weight).

2 A room is 5.3 m by 3.2 m, both to the nearest 10 cm. What is the

   (i) maximum possible area   (ii) minimum possible area?

   (i) Maximum length = 5.35 m and maximum width = 3.25 m
   (length and width can be half of 10 cm (i.e. 5 cm) more or less than given measurements)
   Maximum area = 5.35 × 3.25 = 17.3875 = 17.4 m^2 to 3 s.f.

   (ii) Minimum length = 5.25 m and minimum width = 3.15 m
   Minimum area = 5.25 × 3.15 = 16.5375 = 16.5 m^2 to 3 s.f.

3 A car goes 99 miles, correct to the nearest mile, in $1\frac{1}{2}$ hours, correct to the nearest minute.

   Find the average speed.

   Speed = $\dfrac{\text{distance}}{\text{time}}$

   Highest average speed = $\dfrac{\text{maximum distance}}{\text{minimum time}}$

   = $\dfrac{99.5}{89.5 \div 60}$ (time must be in hours)   = 67 mph to 2 s.f.

   Lowest average speed = $\dfrac{\text{minimum distance}}{\text{maximum time}}$

   = $\dfrac{98.5}{90.5 \div 60}$ = 65 mph to 2 s.f.

Question Bank 10

1 The numbers of students in the six secondary schools in Deeborough are
1200, 1400, 1100, 1000, 1300 and 900, all to the nearest 100.
The minimum number of secondary school pupils in Deeborough is:

a 6850 ☐

b 6900 ☐

c 6600 ☐

d 6750 ☐

Pete runs 1000m (to nearest m) in 40 seconds (to nearest s).

2 What are the maximum and minimum distances Pete could have run?

3 What are Pete's maximum and minimum times?

4 To work out Pete's maximum speed, calculate:

a $\dfrac{\text{minimum distance}}{\text{maximum time}}$ b $\dfrac{\text{maximum distance}}{\text{minimum time}}$

c $\dfrac{\text{minimum distance}}{\text{minimum time}}$ d $\dfrac{\text{maximum distance}}{\text{maximum time}}$

5 Find Pete's maximum speed to 3 s.f.

Squares, square roots, cubes and cube roots

This topic is straightforward and you should be able to get full marks on it.

- The area of this square is $4 \times 4 = 16$.

  4×4 can be written as 4^2 (4 squared)

  $4 \times 4 = 4^2 = 16$

  16 is the **square** of 4.

  16 is a **square number.**

- Use the x^2 key on your calculator to find the square of a number.

- The length of the side of this square is 6.

- The **square root** of 36 is 6.

  $$\sqrt{36} = 6$$

- All positive numbers have two square roots, one is **positive** and one is **negative**.

  The positive square root of 36 is 6. The negative square root is −6.

  $$-6 \times -6 = (-6)^2 = 36$$

- Use the $\sqrt{}$ key on your calculator to find the positive square root of a number.

- The volume of this cube is 27.

  $3 \times 3 \times 3 = 3^3$ (3 cubed)

  The **cube** of 3 is 27.

  27 is a **cube number**.

- Use the x^y key on your calculator to find cubes.

- The length of the side of this cube is 5.

  $$\sqrt[3]{125} = 5$$

- Use the $\sqrt[3]{}$ key to find a cube root.

Question Bank 11

1 What is the negative square root of 196?

2 True or false?

The square of 12.5 lies between 144 and 169.

3 The square root of the square of 19 is ___.

4 The volume of a cube of side 4 units is:

  a 16 ☐

  b 444 ☐

  c 12 ☐

  d 64 ☐

5 Match these numbers with the correct answers.

  a 5^3 ☐   **b** $\sqrt{225}$ ☐   **c** $\sqrt[3]{64}$ ☐   **d** $\left(\sqrt[3]{27}\right)^2$ ☐

  (i) 9   (ii) 15   (iii) 4   (iv) 125

GRADE BOOSTER

Learn the squares and square roots of the numbers from 1 to 15 and the cubes of 2, 3, 4, 5 and 10.

Percentages 1

> Percentages are really quite straightforward. 'Per cent' means 'number of parts per hundred'. If 60% of the students are under fifteen, it means that 60 students in every 100 are under fifteen.

■ Percentages can be written as fractions or decimals.

$$117\frac{1}{2}\% = \frac{117.5}{100} = 1.175$$

■ To change a fraction or a decimal to a percentage, multiply by 100%.

$$\frac{5}{8} = \frac{5}{8} \times 100\% = \frac{500\%}{8} = 62.5\%$$

$$1.85 = 1.85 \times 100\% = 185\%$$

■ To find what percentage one quantity is of another, write a fraction and multiply by 100%.

There are 250 children in a primary school and 131 of them are girls. What percentage is this?

$$\frac{131}{250} \times 100\% = 52\% \text{ to nearest whole number}$$

■ Finding a percentage increase.

If prices are increased by 12%, the new price will be the old price (100%) + the increase (12%), so the new price is 112% of the old price. Multiply the old price by 1.12.

■ Finding a percentage decrease.

If prices are reduced by 5% the new price is the old price (100%) minus the decrease (5%), so the new price is 95% of the old price. Multiply the old price by 0.95.

Question Bank 12

1 To increase by 30% the multiplier is:

   a 1.3 ☐

   b 0.7 ☐

   c 130 ☐

   d 13 ☐

2 Change to percentages:

   a $\frac{3}{8}$

   b 0.55

3 Match each fraction or decimal with the correct percentage.

   a $\frac{2}{3}$ ☐   **b** 0.05 ☐   **c** $\frac{1}{10}$ ☐   **d** 1.5 ☐

   (i) 5%   (ii) 150%   (iii) 10%   (iv) $66\frac{2}{3}$%

4 20% of £132 is:

   a £264 ☐   **c** £2.64 ☐

   b £26.04 ☐   **d** £26.40 ☐

5 The value of a car depreciates 35% in its first year. What is the value of a car, purchased for £12 355, after one year? (Give your answer to the nearest £10.)

GRADE BOOSTER

It's worth learning how to find percentage increases and decreases by the 'multiplier method' as it's quick and, as there are fewer steps, errors are less likely.

Percentages 2

You might find these tricky at first, but if you're careful you shouldn't have any problems. Reverse percentages are used to work out what the original amount was before a percentage increase or decrease was applied.

1   Gina and Mario paid £52.26, including VAT, for a meal at Mussolini's Fish Restaurant. What was the price before VAT at 17.5% was added?

117.5% of price = £52.26

1% of price = $\frac{£52.26}{117.5}$ (Work out 1% – the *unitary* method.)

100% of price = 100 × $\frac{£52.26}{117.5}$

                         (Don't use your calculator until the final stage – your answer will be more accurate.)

= £44.48 to nearest penny   (Always give money to the nearest penny.)

2   When the Puritans were in power they increased the price of beer by 15%. There is an election and the Party People win. They reduce the price of beer by 15%. What is the price now?

The multiplier for a 15% increase is 1.15, so the price will be 1.15 times what it was.

The multiplier for a 15% decrease is 0.85, so the price will be 0.85 times what it was.

The price will be 1.15 × 0.85 = 0.9775 times what it was.

The new price is 97.75% of the original price.

Question Bank 13

1 True or false?

   Prices are increased by 10% and then reduced by 10%. The final price of an article whose original price was £20 will be £20.

2 After a price increase of 5% a car costs £18 690. To find the original price divide by:

   a 0.05   ☐

   b 0.95   ☐

   c 1.05   ☐

   d 0.5   ☐

3 If the VAT rate is 15%, what is the price before VAT of a watch costing £86.25?

4 The number of students at Reedwright's Academy fell by 7% between 1995 and 2000.

   If there were 1432 students in 2000, how many were there in 1995?

5 Last month there was 8.5cm of rain, which was 40% more than the average. What is the average amount of rainfall?

GRADE BOOSTER

Take extra care when you work out the multiplier for a percentage reduction.

Ratio 1

*Don't be put off by this topic. Try to keep it in proportion! A **ratio** is a comparison between two (or more) quantities.*

■ Ratios can be simplified.

My grandmother had 9 children – 3 girls and 6 boys. What was the ratio of boys to girls?

$$Ratio = 6 : 3$$
$$= 2 : 1$$

■ Quantities in a ratio must have the same units.

Sean picked 500g blackberries and Simon picked 1kg. Write this as a ratio.

$$Ratio = 500 : 1000$$
$$= 1 : 2$$

■ Ratios can be changed to fractions, decimals or percentages.

$$2 : 5 = \frac{2}{5} = 2 \div 5 = 0.4 = 40\%$$

■ Map scales are ratios. A scale of 1 : 50000 means 1cm on the map is 50000cm on the ground.

On a map of scale 1 : 50000, two towns are 15cm apart.
What is the actual distance between the towns?

1cm on map = 50000cm on the ground (unitary method)

15cm on the map = 15×50000cm on the ground

$$= \frac{15 \times 50000}{100 \times 1000} = 7.5km$$

■ To share in a given ratio, first find the total number of parts.
Harriet and Lucy share £20 in the ratio 3 : 2. How much does each girl get?

$$3 + 2 = 5 \text{ so divide £20 into 5 parts.}$$

Harriet gets $\frac{3}{5}$ of £20 = £12

Lucy gets $\frac{2}{5}$ of £20 = £8

Question Bank 14

1 Match each ratio with the correct answer.

a 3 : 6 ☐   **b** 18 : 12 ☐   **c** $2\frac{1}{2}$: 15 ☐   **d** 4km : 800m ☐

(i) 1 : 6   (ii) 5 : 1   (iii) 1 : 2   (iv) 3 : 2

2 A road 8km long is 2cm long on a map. The scale of the map is:

a 1 : 80000   ☐

b 1 : 400000   ☐

c 1 : 16000   ☐

d 1 : 40000   ☐

3 Fill in the gaps.

The ratio 11 : 20 is equal to a) $\frac{\quad}{20}$ b) 0.__   c) __%

4 Share £50 between Victoria and Albert in the ratio 3 : 7.

5 True or false?

On a map of scale 1 : 25000 two towns are 12cm apart. The actual distance between the towns is 30km.

GRADE BOOSTER
Remember to use the same units in both parts of a ratio.

Ratio 2

After you've read this page you'll know all you need to know about ratio.

■ The unitary method is useful in ratio problems.

a A recipe for 2 people uses 250g of meat. How much meat is needed for 5 people?

Amount of meat for 1 person = 250 ÷ 2 = 125g   (Find 1 part, then multiply – this is the unitary method.)

Amount for 5 people = 5 × 125 = 625g

b Brass is an alloy of 16 parts copper to 9 parts zinc. If 48kg of copper are used, what is the weight of the final alloy?

Ratio = 16 : 9   (the copper is 16 parts out of 25)

48kg ÷ 16 = 3kg   (1 part)

So 25 parts (the whole) = 25 × 3 = 75kg

■ You can have three or more parts in a ratio.

A house, worth £180000, is left to 3 people in the ratio of their ages. Abbie is 25, Bill is 30 and Cherie is 35. Work out each share.

25 : 30 : 35 = 5 : 6 : 7   (simplify first)

5 + 6 + 7 = 18

So 1 share = £180000 ÷ 18 = £10000

Abbie gets 5 × £10000 = £50000; Bill gets £60000 and Cherie gets £70000.

Question Bank 15

1 Jo needs 300g of flour to make Yorkshire pudding for 6 people.
   For 8 people she needs:

   a 400g ☐   c 600g ☐

   b 350g ☐   d 450g ☐

2 Bronze is 1 part tin to 9 parts copper. How much tin is there in 90kg of
   bronze?

3 Divide 90 in the ratio 1 : 3 : 5.

4 Fill in the gaps.

25%		0.25	1 : 4
$33\frac{1}{3}$	$\frac{1}{3}$	0.3	
	$\frac{4}{5}$	0.8	4 : 5
120%	$1\frac{1}{5}$		6 : 5

Direct proportion

> *Let's start with an example.*
>
> If 1 litre of petrol costs 80p, then 15 litres will cost $15 \times 80p = £12.00$.
>
> *The number of litres of petrol and the cost are in **direct proportion**. The more petrol you buy, the more you pay.*

Examples

1 Bob irons 3 shirts in 17 minutes. How long will it take him to iron 7 shirts?

3 shirts take 17 min

1 shirt takes $\frac{17}{3}$ min   (Work back to 1 – this is the unitary method.)

Don't work this out. Your answer will be more accurate if you save the calculation till the end.

7 shirts take $7 \times \frac{17}{3} = 39.66\dot{6}$

$= 40$ min to nearest minute   (Give the answer to an appropriate degree of accuracy.)

2 If 8 tubes of acrylic paint cost £31.60, how much will 5 tubes cost?

8 tubes cost £31.60

1 tube costs $\frac{£31.60}{8}$ 5 tubes cost $5 \times \frac{£31.60}{8} = £19.75$

3 A tree 16 m high has a shadow 21 m long. How high is a tree with a 12 m shadow?

21 m shadow cast by 16 m tree   (Put the thing you want to find, in this case the height, at the end.)

1 m shadow cast by $(\frac{16}{21})$ m tree

12 m shadow cast by $12 \times \frac{16}{21}$ m tree $= 9.14...$ m

Height of tree $= 9$ m to nearest metre

Question Bank 16

1 Billy can do 20 sums in 15 minutes. How long does it take him to do 10 sums?

2 If 3kg of knitting wool costs £5.40, how much will 5kg cost?

3 A sapphire weighs 11g and is worth £330. The weight of a sapphire worth £540 is:

   a 18g ☐

   b 16.5g ☐

   c 6.7g ☐

   d 20g ☐

4 A ragged rascal can run round 3 rugged rocks in 5 minutes. How many rocks can he run round in $\frac{3}{4}$ hour?

5 My car will go 240 miles on £26 worth of petrol. What is the cost of petrol for a 400-mile journey?

GRADE BOOSTER

You might not see the words 'direct proportion' in a question, but you should recognise the type of problem.

Surds

*A **rational** number is one that can be written as a ratio or fraction. All the integers and all terminating and recurring decimals are rational numbers, e.g.*

$$7 = \frac{7}{1}, \quad 0.53 = \frac{53}{100}, \quad 0.\dot{6} = \frac{2}{3}$$

*An **irrational** number is one that can't be written as a ratio. Numbers like $\sqrt{2}$ and $\sqrt{3}$ are irrational. So are π and numbers such as $5 + \sqrt{3}$.*

*Irrational numbers that contain a square root sign are called **surds**.*

- Calculations with surds.

$\sqrt{5} \times \sqrt{5} = 5$ (The square root of a number multiplied by itself simplifies to the number.)

$2\sqrt{5} \times \sqrt{3} = 2\sqrt{15}$ (You can multiply the square roots together.)

$\sqrt{10} \div \sqrt{2} = \dfrac{\sqrt{10}}{\sqrt{2}} = \dfrac{\sqrt{5} \times \sqrt{2}}{\sqrt{2}} = \sqrt{5}$ (You can cancel square roots.)

$\left(3 + 5\sqrt{2}\right)\left(2 + 3\sqrt{2}\right) = 6 + 10\sqrt{2} + 9\sqrt{2} + 30 = 36 + 19\sqrt{2}$

$\left[5\sqrt{2} \times 3\sqrt{2} = 15 \times \sqrt{2} \times \sqrt{2} = 30\right]$

- Sometimes the surds disappear.

$\left(3 + \sqrt{2}\right)\left(3 - \sqrt{2}\right) = 9 + 3\sqrt{2} - 3\sqrt{2} - 2 = 7$

- Don't find square roots during a calculation. Your answer will be more accurate if you wait till the end.

Example

Find the length c.

$a^2 = 5^2 + 4^2 = 25 + 16 = 41$ (so $a = \sqrt{41}$, *but you don't need to find it*)

$b^2 = a^2 + 4^2 = 41 + 16 = 57$

$c^2 = b^2 + 4^2 = 57 + 16 = 73$ $c = \sqrt{73} = 8.5$ to 2 s.f.

Question Bank 17

1 Which of these is an irrational number?

  a $\frac{2}{9}$ ☐

  b $0.\dot{1}4285\dot{7}$ ☐

  c $\sqrt{9}$ ☐

  d 2π ☐

2 $(4+\sqrt{2})(4-\sqrt{2})$ is equal to:

  a $16+3\sqrt{2}$ ☐

  b 1 ☐

  c $16-3\sqrt{2}$ ☐

  d 14 ☐

3 Find the length x.

  (The answer is an integer.)

4 Simplify $7\left(5+3\sqrt{2}\right)$

5 Fill in the missing numbers.

$$\sqrt{45} \div \sqrt{5} = \frac{\sqrt{9}\times\sqrt{5}}{\sqrt{\underline{\quad}}} = \sqrt{\underline{\quad}} = \underline{\quad}$$

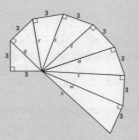

GRADE BOOSTER

Practise manipulating surds – they're quite easy once you get the hang of them.

43

The index laws

This topic's easy once you've learnt the rules.
Indices are a shorthand way of writing products.

$$3 \times 3 \times 3 \times 3 \times 3 = 3^5 \qquad \textit{(3 to the power 5)}$$

$$3^5 \xleftarrow{\text{\quad}} \text{index}$$
$$\text{base}$$

$$3 \times 3 \times 3 \times 3 \times 3 \times 2 \times 2 \times 2 \times 2 = 3^5 \times 2^4$$

- To multiply powers of the same base **add** the indices.
$$3^5 \times 3^3 = (3 \times 3 \times 3 \times 3 \times 3) \times (3 \times 3 \times 3) = 3^8 \quad (5 + 3 = 8)$$

- To divide powers of the same base **subtract** the indices.
$$5^6 \div 5^2 = \frac{5 \times 5 \times 5 \times 5 \times 5 \times 5}{5 \times 5} = 5 \times 5 \times 5 \times 5 = 5^4 \quad (6 - 2 = 4)$$

Look at this sequence: start with 1000 and keep dividing by 10.

1000	100	10	1	$\frac{1}{10}$	$\frac{1}{100}$	$\frac{1}{1000}$

Write the sequence in index form:

10^3	10^2	10^1	10^0	10^{-1}	10^{-2}	10^{-3}

The index goes down by 1 each time you divide by 10.

- Notice that $10^0 = 1$ $\qquad\qquad\qquad 10^{-1} = \frac{1}{10}$ $\quad 10^{-2} = \frac{1}{100} = \frac{1}{10^2}$

- A negative index can be replaced by 'one over'.

$$2^3 \div 2^7 = 2^{-4} = \frac{1}{2^4} = \frac{1}{16}$$

- Using your calculator, use the power key, labelled x^y or y^x.
  e.g. 5^6

  [5] [x^y] [6] [=]   to get 15625.

44

Question Bank 18

1 Simplify

   $7^5 \times 7^7$

2 Which is greater, 6^3 or 3^6?

3 $10^5 \times 10^8 \div 10^{10}$ is:

   a 10^3 ☐

   b 10^{30} ☐

   c 10^4 ☐

   d 10^{-10} ☐

4 Fill in the gaps.

   To multiply powers of the same base _____ the indices.

   To divide powers of the same base _____ the indices.

5 Write in index form:

   $4 \times 4 \times 4 \times 4 \times 4 \times 3 \times 3 \times 2 \times 2 \times 2 \times 2$

6 Match with the correct answer:

   a 10^0 ☐   **b** 2^{-1} ☐

   c $2^3 \times 3^2$ ☐   **d** $2^3 \times 3^3 \div 4^3$ ☐

   (i) $3\frac{3}{8}$ (ii) 1   (iii) 72   (iv) 0.5

Standard index form

Once you get the hang of this topic it can be very useful.

■ Standard index form is a way of writing very large and very small numbers.

a The mass of the Sun is approximately

1 990 000 000 000 000 000 000 000 000 000 kg

$$= 1.99 \times 10^{30} \text{kg}$$

b The mass of a hydrogen atom is about

0.000 000 000 000 000 000 000 001 67 g

$$= 1.67 \times 10^{-24} \text{g}$$

■ To write a number in standard index form, express it as a number between 1 and 10 multiplied by the appropriate power of 10.

Examples

1 $730\ 000 = 7.3 \times 10^5$

Put the decimal point between the 7 and the 3 and count how many places it has to be moved to the right to get back to the original number. So the power of 10 is 5.

2 $0.000\ 000\ 000\ 405 = 4.05 \times 10^{-10}$

Put the decimal point after the first non-zero number and count how many places it has to be moved to the left to get back to the original number. So the power of 10 is −10.

■ Numbers in standard index form can be multiplied and divided using the index laws.

$(2.7 \times 10^3) \times (8 \times 10^7) = 21.6 \times 10^{10} = 2.16 \times 10^{11}$
(both answers are correct, but the second is in standard index form)

$(5.8 \times 10^8) \div (3.1 \times 10^6) = 1.9 \times 10^2$ to 2 s.f.

Question Bank 19

1   The speed of light is 300 000 000 m/s. Write this in standard index form.

2   $(7 \times 10^5) \times (3 \times 10^{-8})$ in standard index form is:

a 2.1×10^{-3} ☐

b 21×10^{-3} ☐

c 2.1×10^{-2} ☐

d 2.1×10^{-4} ☐

3   Which is greater?

a) $(6 \times 10^4) \times (5 \times 10^3)$ or   b) $(6 \times 10^4) \div (5 \times 10^{-4})$

4   Your heart beats about 70 times a minute. If you live to 70, how many beats will your heart make? Give your answer in standard form rounded to 2 s.f.

5   Match the numbers.

a   2.4 ☐   b   0.0024 ☐   c   2400 ☐   d   0.024 ☐

(i) 2.4×10^3 (ii) 2.4×10^{-3} (iii) 2.4×10^0 (iv) 2.4×10^{-2}

GRADE BOOSTER

Remember to check you have the correct index after changing a number to standard index form.

Standard index form on your calculator

Lots of students get in a muddle over this. We'll make sure you're not one of them. Most calculators have an EXP (or EE) key for standard form.

To enter 5.8×10^9 in your calculator, key in

| 5.8 | | EXP | | 9 |

The display will show

| 5.8 | 09 | or | 5.8 | **E** | 9 |

To calculate $5.8 \times 10^9 \div 6.2 \times 10^{-4}$ key in

| 5.8 | EXP | 9 | ÷ | 6.2 | EXP | +/- | 4 | = |

The answer is 9.3548×10^{12}.

Example

Cosmologists think that the Big Bang, when the universe began to expand, occurred 20 thousand million years ago. How many days ago was that? Write your answer in standard form.

Number of days $= 20 \times 10^3 \times 10^6 \times 365$ days

Key in:

| 20 | × | 10^9 | × | 365 | = |

to get:

| 73 | 12 |

The Big Bang occurred $73 \times 10^{12} = 7.3 \times 10^{13}$ days ago.

Question Bank 20

1 A calculator display shows

    4.31   07

    Write this as an ordinary number.

2 Light travels at 3×10^5 km/s. The number of kilometres light travels in one year, to 2 s.f., is:

    a 9.5×10^{12} ☐

    b 1.6×10^{11} ☐

    c 3.9×10^{11} ☐

    d 2.6×10^{10} ☐

3 Work out $(8.5 \times 10^{12}) \div 3500$.

4 My newspaper is made up of 9 sheets, each measuring $75\,\text{cm} \times 60\,\text{cm}$. If 100 000 papers are printed, what is the total area of paper used? Give you answer to 2 s.f. in standard form.

5 If the number displayed on a calculator as

    6.83   −14

    is written in full, how many zeros follow the decimal point?

GRADE BOOSTER

Practise standard index form on your calculator until you're confident at using the EXP key. It's easy to get full marks on these questions.

Compound interest

*Start by going through the example and then using your calculator to check the answer. When money is invested (saved) it earns **interest**. At the end of the year the interest is added to the original sum invested (the principal), and the next year's interest is paid on the new principal. This is **compound interest**.*

Example

Marie invests £500 for 3 years. The rate of interest is 6% per annum (each year). Calculate the value of Marie's investment at the end of 3 years.

First year's interest = 6% × £500 = 0.06 × £500 = £30

After 1 year, principal = £500 + £30 = £530

Second year's interest = 6% × £530 = 0.06 × £530 = £31 .80

After 2 years, principal = £530 + £31.80 = £561.80

Third year's interest = 6% × £531.80 = 0.06 × £531.80
                       = £33.71 to nearest penny

After 3 years Marie has £561.80 + £33.71 = £595.51

■ Using a calculator

The principal increases by 6% each year, so you can multiply by 1.06 to find the new principal at the end of 1 year. After 3 years the original principal has been multiplied by
$1.06 \times 1.06 \times 1.06 = 1.06^3$.

So, after 3 years the value of Marie's investment = £500 × 1.06^3 = £595.51 to nearest penny.

You can do this on your calculator, using the power key (labelled x^y or y^x). Key in

| 500 | × | 1.06 | x^y | 3 | = |

Question Bank 21

1 Match each rate of interest with the correct multiplier.

    a 3% ☐   **b** 10% ☐   **c** $4\frac{1}{2}$ % ☐   **d** $5\frac{1}{4}$ % ☐

    (i) 1.1   (ii) 1.045   (iii) 1.0525   (iv) 1.03

2 How much interest is paid on £1000 at $5\frac{1}{2}$ % for 1 year?

    a £5.50 ☐   **c** £1005.50 ☐

    b £55 ☐   **d** £550 ☐

3 Rashid borrows £2000 at 7% for 2 years. How much does he owe at the end of the 2 years?

4 The value of a new car, costing £15000, depreciates by 15% every year. To find the value of the car after 3 years, multiply £15000 by:

    a 1.15 ☐   **c** 0.85 ☐

    b 1.15^3 ☐   **d** 0.85^3 ☐

5 A bank pays 5% interest on £5000 in a deposit account. How many years will it take to double the money? (Use a calculator.)

    a 2 ☐   **c** 15 ☐

    b 10 ☐   **d** 20 ☐

GRADE BOOSTER

Practise working out the multipliers for percentage rates containing fractions.

Compound measures

This is a straightforward topic as long as you keep a clear head! Speed and density are compound measures.

Speed = distance ÷ time   Distance = speed × time
Time = distance ÷ speed

This triangle helps you remember the formulae.

To find *D*, cover *D* and you get *ST*

To find *S*, cover S and you get *D/T*

To find *T*, cover *T* and you get *D/S*

Example

Zoë runs a kilometre in 5 minutes. What is her speed in m/s?

$$\text{Speed} = \frac{\text{distance}}{\text{time}} = \frac{1000}{5}\,\text{m/min} = \frac{1000}{5 \times 60}\,\text{m/s} = 3.3\,\text{m/s (to 2 s.f.)}$$

You might see a speed of 50 km/h written as 50 km h⁻¹.

Density = mass/volume   Mass = density × volume   Volume = mass/density

Use this triangle to remember the formulae.

Example

A cuboid, 10 cm long, 7.5 cm wide and 5 cm high, is made of a metal of density 15 g/cm³.

Find the mass of the cuboid.

Volume = 10 × 7.5 × 5

      = 375 cm³

Mass = density × volume

      = 15 × 375

      = 5625 g

      = 5.6 kg to 2 s.f.

Question Bank 22

1 To change 6 km/h to m/s:

   a Multiply by 1000 and divide by 60

   b Divide by 1000 and multiply by 60

   c Multiply by 1000 and divide by 360

   d Multiply by 100 and divide by 360

2 A bird flies 185 m in 5 seconds. Find its speed in m/s.

3 Rashid jogs at 8 km/h. How far does he go in 30 minutes?

4 A cuboid is 5 cm × 5 cm × 10 cm. It weighs 1 kg. Its density is:

   a 0.004 g/cm^3

   b 4 g/cm^3

   c 40 g/cm^3

   d 0.04 g/cm^3

5 The volume of a metal ball is 1.1 cm^3. The density is 9.0 g/cm^3.
   What is the mass of the ball to 2 s.f?

GRADE BOOSTER

Be extra careful with the units in compound measure questions.

Inverses and reciprocals

> *Inverses undo things.*
> **Subtraction** is the inverse of **addition** and vice versa.
> **Multiplication** and **division** are inverse operations.

Numbers have inverses. The inverse of 2 is −2 for addition
(because $2 + (-2) = 0$) and $\frac{1}{2}$ for multiplication because $\frac{1}{2} \times 2 = 1$

2^{-1} or $\frac{1}{2}$ is the **reciprocal** or **multiplicative inverse** of 2.

- Any number × its reciprocal = 1

  Every number, except 0, has a reciprocal. Zero has no reciprocal because
  whatever it is multiplied by it's still 0!

- To find the reciprocal of a fraction turn it upside-down.

- To find the reciprocal of a decimal, first write it as a fraction.

  What are the reciprocals of $\frac{4}{5}$, 0.2, 17 and $2\frac{3}{4}$?

  Reciprocal of $\frac{4}{5} = \frac{5}{4}$.

  $0.2 = \frac{2}{10}$, so reciprocal of 0.2 is $\frac{10}{2} = 5$.

  Reciprocal of 17 = $\frac{1}{17}$.

  $2\frac{3}{4} = \frac{11}{4}$, so reciprocal of $2\frac{3}{4} = \frac{4}{11}$.

Your calculator has a key labelled $1/x$ or x^{-1}.

To find 7^{-1}, the reciprocal of 7, key

| 7 | | $1/x$ | | = |

You get 0.1428571429. This is an approximation. The result is rounded to
the number of decimal places on your display. In fraction form, the
reciprocal is 1/7, which is the exact value.

Multiplication is the inverse of division so instead of dividing by a fraction
you can multiply by its reciprocal.

- To divide by a fraction, multiply by its reciprocal. $\frac{3}{4} \div \frac{7}{8} = \frac{3}{4} \times \frac{8}{7} = \frac{6}{7}$

Question Bank 23

1 Match each number with its reciprocal.

   a $\frac{3}{20}$ ☐   **b** 2.5 ☐   **c** $\frac{5}{8}$ ☐   **d** 0.6 ☐

   (i) $\frac{5}{3}$ (ii) 1.6   (iii) 0.4   (iv) $\frac{20}{3}$

2 Which number does not have a reciprocal?

3 True or false?

   a $5^{-1} = 0.2$

   b $5^{-2} = \frac{1}{10}$

4 The reciprocal of 25 is 0.04. What is the reciprocal of 0.04?

5 What is the reciprocal of 0.3?

GRADE BOOSTER

Use the reciprocal in fraction form if possible, as it's more accurate.

SECTION 2 ALGEBRA

Expressions and equations

> *The normal rules of arithmetic apply when you do algebra.*

- $3y - 8 = 7$ is an **equation.** It has an equals sign. It is only true when y is 5.

- $3y - 8$ is an **expression**. It has two **terms**: $3y$ and -8. There is no equals sign.

- $2(a - 3) \equiv 2a - 6$ is an **identity**. It is true for all values of a. Try it! The sign $\equiv$ means 'is identical to'.

- $V = IR$ is a **formula**. You can use it to find values of V for various values of I and R.

Manipulating expressions

- You can collect up **like terms**, e.g.
$$3x + 7y - 2x^2 + 5xy - 5x + x^2 = -x^2 - 2x + 5xy + 7y$$

- You can **expand** (multiply out) brackets, e.g.
$$a(b + d) = ab + ad$$
$$(2x + 1)(3x - 4) = 6x^2 - 5x - 4$$

To multiply two brackets with two terms each, use 'FOIL' – multiply together the two First ($2x \times 3x$), the two Outer ($2x \times -4$), the two Inner ($1 \times 3x$) and the Last two terms (1×-4): $6x^2 - 8x + 3x - 4 = 6x^2 - 5x - 4$

- You can **factorise**.
$$5pq + 10p^2 = 5p(q + 2p)$$

- You can **cancel**.
$$\frac{2(x + 1)(x + 3)}{x + 1} = 2(x + 3)$$

Question Bank 24

1 Which of these is an identity?

  a $5x(2x^2 - 4x + 7) \equiv 10x^3 - 20x^2 + 35x$ ☐

  b $3a^2 - 5a + 2 = 6$ ☐

  c $E = mc^2$ ☐   **d** $a^2 + b^2 + c^2$ ☐

2 Complete the factors:

  $3x^2 + 6x = 3\_\_ (x + \_\_)$

3 Match each expression with the correct answer.

  a $(y - 2)(y + 3)$ ☐   **c** $(y + 2)(y + 3)$ ☐

  b $(y - 2)(y - 3)$ ☐   **d** $(y + 2)(y - 3)$ ☐

  (i) $y^2 + 5y + 6$ (iii) $y^2 - y - 6$

  (ii) $y^2 + y - 6$ (iv) $y^2 - 5y + 6$

4 Simplify:

  $\dfrac{6ab(c - d)(c + d)}{2ab^2 (d + c)}$

5 $(x + y)(x - y)$ is identical to:

  a $x^2 + 2xy + y^2$ ☐   **c** $x^2 - 2xy - y^2$ ☐

  b $x^2 - 2xy + y^2$ ☐   **d** $x^2 - y^2$ ☐

6 If $v^2 = u^2 + 2as$, find the value of v when $u = 20$, $a = 3$ and $s = 5$.

GRADE BOOSTER

'Simplify' means 'do something', such as 'collect up like terms', 'cancel' or 'expand'. Don't let the algebra scare you. Start by writing down the given expression. Inspiration often strikes as you do this!

Setting up equations

a What are the angles of this triangle?

$a + 2a + 3a = 180°$ (angle sum of triangle is 180°)

$6a = 180°$

$a = 30°$

The angles are 30°, 60° and 90°.

b How long is this room if its area is 20 m²
and its width is 3.2 m?

$x \times 3.2 = 20$

$x = \dfrac{20}{3.2} = 6.3\,\text{m to 2 s.f.}$

The length of the room is 6.3 m.

c Marika was 26 when her son, Ali, was born in 1988. Now she is 3 times as old as Ali. What year is it now?

If Ali is now x years old, then Marika is $26 + x$.

$26 + x = 3 \times x$

$26 = 2x$

$x = 13$

The year is now $1988 + 13 = 2001$.

Question Bank 25

1 Three consecutive whole numbers add up to 150. If the smallest number is x, write down and simplify the equation you would use to find the numbers.

2 Write an equation to find the size of the angles in this triangle.

3 The perimeter of this rectangle is 30 cm.

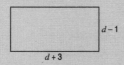

Which is the right equation to find the value of d?

a $2(d-1)(d+3) = 30$ ☐   **c** $2(d-1) + 2(d+3) = 30$ ☐

b $(d-1)(d+3) = 30$ ☐   **d** $2d + 2 = 30$ ☐

4 The product of two consecutive even numbers (two consecutive even numbers multiplied) is 12 more than the square of the smaller number. The equation to find the numbers is:

a $x(x+2) - 12 = x^2$ ☐   **c** $x(x+2) + x^2 = 12$ ☐

b $x(x+2) = x^2 - 12$ ☐   **d** $x^2 - x(x+2) = 12$ ☐

GRADE BOOSTER

You can do some of these problems without setting up an equation – but you get the marks for the equation.

Formulae

If you find that formulae can be tricky, the examples here should be some help.

- **Using a formula**. The volume of a cylinder is found by using the formula $V = \pi r^2 h$. What is the volume of a cylinder with radius 1.5 cm and height 5.6 cm?

  $V = \pi \times 1.5^2 \times 5.6 = 40 \, \text{cm}^3$ to 2 s.f.

- The **subject** is the letter before the equals sign. In the example above, the subject is V. Sometimes you are asked to make a different letter the subject.

a Make h the subject of the formula $V = \pi r^2 h$.

  $\pi r^2 h = V$ (change over the sides)

  $h = \dfrac{V}{\pi r^2}$ (divide both sides by πr^2)

  h is now the subject.

  Notice that you use the same methods as when solving equations.

b Make r the subject of the formula $V = \pi r^2 h$

  $\pi r^2 h = V$ $r^2 = \dfrac{V}{\pi h}$ $r = \sqrt{\dfrac{V}{\pi h}}$ (square root both sides)

- You might be asked to write a formula.

c After the floods Noah hired a dehumidifier at a basic charge of £50 plus £5.50 per day. Write a formula for the cost, C, of hiring a dehumidifier for n days.

  Cost $= £50 + n \times £5.50$ (It helps to write the formula in words first.)

  $C = 50 + 5.5n$ (Remember – no units in formulae, and put the numbers (5.5) before the letters (n).)

Question Bank 26

1   The formula $F = ma$ tells us that force = mass × acceleration.

If a mass of 12kg has an acceleration of $1.5\,\text{m/s}^2$, what is the force?

   a 1.8 N ☐   **c** 18 N ☐

   b 8 N ☐   **d** 10.5 N ☐

2   If you write the formula $y = mx + c$ with x as the subject, the formula is:

   a $mx = c - y$ ☐   **c** $mx = y - c$ ☐

   b $x = \frac{y-c}{m}$ ☐   **d** $mx + c = y$ ☐

3   Einstein's famous formula in the theory of relativity is $E = mc^2$.

   When $m = 0.1\,\text{g}$ and $c = 3 \times 10^8\,\text{m/s}$, what is E?

4   A car salesman earns £200 per week plus commission of £80 for each
   car he sells.

   Find a formula for his wage, W, in a week when he sells n cars.

5   Write a formula for the height, h, of a triangle with area A and base b.

GRADE BOOSTER

Use the same rules with formulae as for equations. The most
important rule is *'Do the same to both sides'*.

Sequences

■ A **sequence** is a list of numbers with a pattern. Often the pattern is easy to spot,
e.g. 1, 4, 7, 10, ...

■ The *term-to-term* rule for this sequence is 'add 3'.
First term, 1; add 3 = second term, 4; and so on.

■ You can use a *position-to-term* rule to write a sequence. Here's how.
Write down the first five terms of a sequence with nth term, $4 + 3n$.
For the first term $n = 1$, so first term = $4 + 3 \times 1 = 7$
For the second term $n = 2$, so second term = $4 + 3 \times 2 = 10$
Similarly, the third term = $4 + 3 \times 3 = 13$, and so on.
The sequence is 7, 10, 13, 16, 19, ...

■ You can find the rule for a sequence by writing down the *differences between the terms*, like this.
What is the position-to-term rule for the sequence: 3, 5, 7, 9, 11, ...?

Position (n)	1	2	3	4	5
Term	3	5	7	9	11

(Write down each term underneath its position, n.)

The terms go up by 2 each time, so write down the sequence $2n$.

$2n$	2	4	6	8	10

Each term in the original sequence is 1 more than in the $2n$ sequence.
So the position-to-term rule is $2n + 1$.

Question Bank 27

1 Write down the next two terms of the sequence

   200, 100, 50, ...

2 The first term of a sequence is 243. The term-to-term rule is '÷ 3'.
   What are the next four terms of the sequence?

3 The position-to-term rule for this sequence

   7   16   25   34   43

   is:

   a $9n$ ☐

   b $n \times n$ ☐

   c $(n \times n) - 2$ ☐

   d $9n - 2$ ☐

4 What is the 10th term of the sequence with nth term $2n + 5$?

5 The first odd number is 1. Write down the nth odd number.

   (Hint: Write the sequence of odd numbers first.)

GRADE BOOSTER

Don't be put off by 'the nth term'. It just means 'any old term in the sequence'.

Index notation

When you write $3 \times 3 \times 3 \times 3$ as 3^4, you're using index notation. The rules are the same as in arithmetic.

- Here is a reminder.

    $a^m \times a^n = a^{m+n}$ (to multiply powers, add the indices)

    $a^m \div a^n = a^{m-n}$ (to divide powers, subtract the indices)

    $(a^m)^n = a^{m \times n} = a^{mn}$

    $a^0 = 1$

    $a^{-1} = \dfrac{1}{a}$

    $\dfrac{1}{a}$ is called the **reciprocal** of a. A number $\times$ its reciprocal $= 1$ ($\dfrac{1}{a} \times a = 1$)

    $a^{-n} = \dfrac{1}{a^n}$

- Here are the rules in action.

a $x^2 y^2 \times x^3 y = x^5 y^3$

b $(3x^2)^3 = 27x^6$ (Remember to cube the 3 as well as the x^2.)

c $\dfrac{6p^2qr^3}{2pq^2r} = \dfrac{3pr^2}{q}$

d $x^2(2x^2 - 3xy + y^2) = 2x^4 - 3x^3y + x^2y^2$

Find the value of these expressions when $a = 4$ and $b = -3$.

a $3a^2 + 2b$ **b** $2b^3$

a $3a^2 + 2b = 3 \times 4^2 + 2 \times -3 = 48 - 6 = 42$

b $2b^3 = 2 \times (-3)^3 = 2 \times -27 = -54$

Question Bank 28

1 If $a = 4$, $b = -1$ and $c = -2$, the value of $a^2 (b - c)$ is:

  a -10 ☐

  b 16 ☐

  c -48 ☐

  d -24 ☐

2 If $x = -3$ and $y = 5$, evaluate $y - x^2$.

3 What is the area of this rectangle?

$2x + y$

$3x$

4 $3a^4b^2 \times 2ab^5$ simplifies to:

  a $6a^5b^7$ ☐

  b $5a^5b^7$ ☐

  c $6a^4b^{10}$ ☐

  d $32a^4b^{10}$ ☐

5 Simplify $8x^7 \div 2x^3$.

GRADE BOOSTER

Learn the rules and remember that anything to the power $0 = 1$.

Factorising

*A factor in algebra is just like a factor in arithmetic. It's a term that divides exactly into another term. **Factorise** just means find the factors. Let's start by looking at some easy ones.*

■ Some expressions have a common factor.

$x^3y + 2xy^2 = xy(x^2 + 2y)$ (common factor is xy)

■ **Factorising by grouping**

$xy + xz + wy + wz = xy + xz \mid + wy + wz$

(Divide into pairs. x is a common factor in the first pair and w is a common factor in second pair.)

$= x(y + z) + w(y + z)$ (($y + z$) is a common factor)

$= (y + z)(x + w)$

■ **Factorising quadratic expressions**

When you expand $(x + 4)$ $(x + 5)$ you get $x^2 + 9x + 20$, which is a *quadratic* expression.

If you do the process in reverse you're factorising a quadratic expression.

a $x^2 + 8x + 12$ (Find two numbers that multiply to give 12 and add to give 8: 6 and 2.)

So $x^2 + 8x + 12 = (x + 2)(x + 6)$ (Check your answer by multiplying the brackets.)

b $x^2 - 4x - 12$ (Find two numbers that multiply to give -12 and add to give -4: -6 and 2.)

So $x^2 - 4x - 12 = (x - 6)(x + 2)$ (Check by multiplying.)

Question Bank 29

1 Factorise $10ab + 15ad$.

2 True or false?

   One of the factors of $xk - xm - kz + mz$ is $(k - m)$.

3 The factors of $x^2 - 8x + 12$ are:

   a $(x + 6)(x - 2)$ ☐

   b $(x - 2)(x - 6)$ ☐

   c $(x - 10)(x + 2)$ ☐

   d $(x - 6)(x + 2)$ ☐

4 Factorise $6ax + 2bx + 3ay + by$.

5 The highest common factor of the expression $x^2yz + xy^2z + xyz^2$ is:

   a xy ☐

   b xz ☐

   c yz ☐

   d xyz ☐

GRADE BOOSTER

Practise spotting common factors. If you can simplify an expression by factorising, it often leads to the result you need in a problem.

Linear equations

> When you work with equations, remember the golden rule, 'Do the same thing to both sides', and you won't go wrong.

The simplest equations are linear equations, e.g. $x + 5 = 17$.

This is how you solve them.

a $3x - 5 = 16$ (add 5 to each side)

- The aim is to get the x-term on its own on one side of the equation.

     $3x = 21$ (divide each side by 3)

     $x = 7$

b $2(x + 3) = 4$ (expand the brackets)

     $2x + 6 = 4$ (subtract 6 from each side)

     $2x = -2$ (divide each side by 2)

     $x = -1$

c $\dfrac{2x}{3} = 8$ (multiply each side by 3)

- Always clear the fractions first

     $2x = 24$ (divide each side by 2)

     $x = 12$

d $4x - 3 = 7x - 12$ (subtract $4x$ from each side)

     $-3 = 3x - 12$ (add 12 to each side)

     $9 = 3x$ (divide each side by 3)

     $3 = x$ (turn equation round so that x is on the left)

     $x = 3$

e $\dfrac{1}{2}(x + 1) = \dfrac{1}{5}(2x - 3)$ (multiply each side by 10)

- Always get rid of the fractions at the start.

     $5(x + 1) = 2(2x - 3)$ (expand the brackets)

     $5x + 5 = 4x - 6$ (subtract 5 from each side)

     $5x = 4x - 11$ (subtract $4x$ from each side)

     $x = -11$

Question Bank 30

1 The solution to the equation $4(x - 1) = 3x + 2$ is:

   a 2 ☐

   b 4 ☐

   c −5 ☐

   d 6 ☐

2 Solve the equation $\frac{1}{2}x = 8$

3 Match each equation with its solution.

   a $15 + 6x = 3$ ☐

   c $\frac{x}{4} = 2$ ☐

   b $\frac{3x}{2} = 18$ ☐

   d $3x - 7 = -10$ ☐

   (i) −8   (ii) −1   (iii) 12   (iv) −2

4 Which step is wrong?

   (i) $10x - (2x - 3) = 21$ ☐   (iv) $8x = 24$ ☐

   (ii) $10x - 2x - 3 = 21$ ☐   (v) $x = 3$ ☐

   (iii) $8x - 3 = 21$ ☐

5 Solve the equation $a - 3 = 3a + 7$.

GRADE BOOSTER

Always check your solution by substituting in the original equation.
The two sides should be equal to the same number. If they're not,
check your working. It's all too easy to make a mistake in the
working somewhere along the line.

Straight-line graphs 1

> *A straight-line graph is exactly what it says. It can be horizontal, vertical or slanting, but it's got to be straight!*

The graphs of equations such as $y = 3x - 2$ (with no x^2 or higher powers) are straight lines.

Here's how to draw the graph of $y = 2x + 1$.

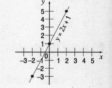

Find three points on the line.

When $x = 0$, $y = 1$. (Points where $x = 0$ and $y = 0$ are often easy to work out.)

When $x = 2$, $y = 5$.

When $x = -2$, $y = -3$.

The three points line are $(0, 1)$, $(2, 5)$, $(-2, -3)$.

(Two points are enough to fix a straight line, but as a check, calculate a third point.)

Draw x- and y-axes and choose suitable scales.

Plot the three points and join them with a straight line.

Plot graphs of these equations.

a $x + y = 5$

When $x = 0$, $y = 5$.

When $x = 5$, $y = 0$.

When $x = 1$, $y = 4$.

Three points on the line are $(0, 5)$, $(5, 0)$, $(1, 4)$.

b $2y = x - 1$

When $x = 0$, $y = -\frac{1}{2}$.

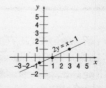

When $x = 1$, $y = 0$.

When $x = 3$, $y = 1$.

Three points on the line are $(0, -\frac{1}{2})$, $(1, 0)$, $(3, 1)$.

Question Bank 31

1 Fill in the missing coordinates for the equation $y = 3x - 5$.

   a $(1, \_)$ **b** $(\_, -5)$ **c** $(2, \_)$

2 Which of these is *not* the equation of a straight line?

   a $y = x^2 - 1$ ☐   **c** $2x - 3 = y$ ☐

   b $2y = 3x + 4$ ☐   **d** $2x + 3 = y - 1$ ☐

3 Which of these points is *not* on the line $2x + y = 7$?

   a $(0, 7)$ ☐

   b $(6, 1)$ ☐

   c $(-1, 9)$ ☐

   d $(3\frac{1}{2}, 0)$ ☐

4 Match the points with the equations.

   a $y = 3x - 4$ ☐   **c** $2y + 3 = 3x - 1$ ☐

   b $x + y = 4$ ☐   **d** $3x - 2y = 8$ ☐

   (i) $(1, -1)$ (ii) $(1, -\frac{1}{2})$ (iii) $(2, -1)$ (iv) $(1, 3)$

5 Find the coordinates of the points where the line $y + 2x = 4$ crosses the x- and y-axes.

GRADE BOOSTER

If your three points don't make a straight line, check them all to find out which one is wrong.

Straight-line graphs 2

Read this page and try the questions. This topic is easy once you know the basics. If a straight-line equation is written in the form $y = mx + c$, i.e. with y as the subject, you can write down the gradient of the line and the intercept the line makes on the y-axis.

■ The **gradient** of a straight line tells you how steep it is. To work out the gradient, find how many units the line **rises** for each unit it **runs** across the page.

For the line $y = \frac{1}{2}x - 2$, **gradient** $= \dfrac{\textbf{rise}}{\textbf{run}} = \dfrac{1}{2}$

For the line $y = -3x + 1$, **gradient** $= \dfrac{\textbf{rise}}{\textbf{run}} = \dfrac{3}{-1} = -3$

■ The gradient is m, the coefficient of x (i.e. the number of xs) in the equation.

■ The **intercept** is the distance from the origin where the line cuts the y-axis.

The line $y = \frac{1}{2}x - 2$ cuts the y-axis at $(0, -2)$. The y-intercept is -2.

The line $y = -3x + 1$ cuts the y-axis at $(0, 1)$. The y-intercept is 1.

■ The intercept of each line is c, the constant term (the number), in the equation.

Now try sketching a graph of $x + y = 5$.

First rearrange the equation so that y is the subject.

$y = -x + 5$:
gradient $= -1$, intercept $= 5$

Question Bank 32

1 Find the coordinates of the points where the line $x + y = 3$ crosses the x- and y-axes.

2 Match the equations with the graphs.

a ☐   b ☐   c ☐   d ☐

(i) $y = x - 2$ (ii) $y = 2 - x$ (iii) $y = x + 2$ (iv) $2y = x$

3 Which of these lines are parallel? (Hint: Find the gradients.)

a $y = 2x + 3$ ☐   c $y = x + 3$ ☐

b $y = 3x + 2$ ☐   d $y = 2x + 1$ ☐

4 Choose the correct answer.

The line $3y = 4x - 2$ has:

a gradient 4, intercept 2 ☐   c gradient $\frac{4}{3}$, intercept $-\frac{2}{3}$ ☐

b gradient 4, intercept -2 ☐   d gradient $\frac{4}{3}$, intercept $\frac{2}{3}$ ☐

5 Find the gradient of the line AB

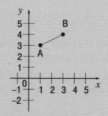

GRADE BOOSTER

Practise rearranging equations with y as the subject so that you can spot the gradient and intercept.

Simultaneous equations 1

> *After you've read this page you'll be on the way to becoming an expert.*

Two equations with one solution are called simultaneous equations, e.g.
$5x + 2y = 8$ and $3x - 2y = 8$

These are linear equations. Their graphs are straight lines. The coordinates of the point where the lines cross is the *solution* of the equations.

However, instead of drawing a graph you can find the solution by algebra. Here's how.

$5x + 2y = 8$ (1)   (Number the equations so that you can refer to them.)

$3x - 2y = 8$ (2)

Add the equations (1) and (2) (so that the y-terms will disappear).

$8x = 16$

$x = 2$

Substitute 2 for x in equation (1) (to find y).

$5 \times 2 + 2y = 8$

$10 + 2y = 8$

$2y = -2$

$y = -1$

Check by putting $x = 2$ and $y = -1$ in one of the original equations:
$5 \times 2 + 2 \times -1 = 10 - 2 = 8$

So the solution, $x = 2$, $y = -1$ is correct.

Question Bank 33

1 What is the solution to the simultaneous equations on the graph?

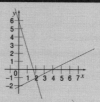

2 The solution to the equations $5x + 2y = 13$, $2x + 6y = 26$ is $x = 1$, $y = 4$.
Where do the lines cross?

3 The solution to the equations $3x + y = 5$ and $6x + 2y = 15$ is:

a $x = 1$, $y = 2$ ☐

b $x = 2$, $y = 1.5$ ☐

c $x = 1$, $y = 4.5$ ☐

d None of these ☐

4 The solution to this pair of simultaneous equations:

$3x + 2y = 13$ (1)

$2x - 2y = -3$ (2)

is:

a $x = 3\frac{1}{2}$, $y = 2$ ☐   c $x = 3\frac{1}{5}$, $y = 2$ ☐

b $x = 2$, $y = 3\frac{1}{2}$ ☐   d $x = 1$, $y = 5$ ☐

5 Solve the equations $x + y = 7$, $x - y = 1$.

GRADE BOOSTER

This method gives you the *exact solution* of the simultaneous equations. The solution found by drawing a graph may not be exact. It depends on how accurately the graph can be read.

Simultaneous equations 2

Here we're going to develop the topic of simultaneous equations a bit further.

In the examples on page 74, the y-terms were eliminated by simply adding the two equations. Sometimes, however, you need to adjust one or both of the equations before you can eliminate the x- or the y-terms.

Here's how you do it.

Solve the following.

a $4x + 5y = 2$ (1) $2x + 3y = 4$ (2)

Multiply eqn (2) by 2 (to get $4x$ in both equations).

$$4x + 6y = 8 \quad (3)$$

Subtract eqn (1) from eqn (3).

$$-\underline{(4x + 5y = 2)} \quad (1)$$
$$y = 6$$

Substitute 6 for y in eqn (1).

$4x + 30 = 2$ $4x = -28$ $x = -7$

Check by putting $x = -7$ and $y = 6$ in eqn (2).

$$2 \times -7 + 3 \times 6 = 4$$

So the solution is $x = -7$, $y = 6$

b $3x + 2y = 7$ (1) $\times 3$ (both equations have to be adjusted)

$2x - 3y = -4$ (2) $\times 2$

$9x + 6y = 21$ (3)

$+\underline{4x - 6y = -8}$ (4)   (add equations (3) and (4))

$13x = 13$

$x = 1$

Substitute 1 for x in eqn (1).

$3 + 2y = 7$ $2y = 4$ $y = 2$

Check in eqn (2)

$2 \times 1 - 3 \times 2 = -4$

So the solution is $x = 1$, $y = 2$.

Question Bank 34

1 Choose the correct answer.

To solve this pair of simultaneous equations:

$3x + 2y = 11$ (1) $\qquad$ $6x - y = -3$ (2)

a Multiply eqn (1) by 2 and eqn (2) by 2 and add $\quad\square$

b Multiply eqn (2) by 2 and add $\quad\square$

c Multiply eqn (2) by 2 and subtract $\quad\square$

d Multiply eqn (1) by 2 and subtract $\quad\square$

2 Solve the equations:

$a + b = -1$ $\qquad$ $b - a = -5$

3 Match each pair of equations with its solution.

a $2x + y = 5$ $\qquad$ **b** $x + 3y = 7$ $\qquad$ **c** $2x + y = -3$

$\quad x + 3y = 5$ $\square$ $\qquad$ $2y - x = 3$ $\square$ $\qquad$ $x - y = -3$ $\square$

(i) $x = 1, y = 2$ $\qquad$ (ii) $x = 2, y = 1$ $\qquad$ (iii) $x = -2, y = 1$

4 The solution to the simultaneous equations

$x + 2y = 1$ and $2x + 3y = 4$ is:

a $x = -2, y = 5$ $\square$ $\quad$ **c** $x = \dfrac{1}{2}, y = 1$ $\square$

b $x = 1, y = 2$ $\square$ $\quad$ **d** $x = 5, y = -2$ $\square$

GRADE BOOSTER

To eliminate one of the variables, multiply one or both equations by a number that gives you the same amount of xs or ys in both equations.

Factorising quadratics

A quadratic equation that can be factorised can be solved easily. Here are some useful tricks.

Let's look at some quadratic expressions.

$$a^2 + 2ab + b^2 = a^2 + ab + ab + b^2 = a(a + b) + b(a + b) = (a + b)(a + b)$$

$$a^2 - 2ab + b^2 = a^2 - ab - ab + b^2 = a(a - b) - b(a - b) = (a - b)(a - b)$$

$$a^2 - b^2 = a^2 + ab - ab - b^2 = a(a + b) - b(a + b) = (a + b)(a - b)$$

Learn these three results. The last one, known as '*a square minus a square*' or '*the difference of two squares*', is particularly useful.

Here's an example.

$$25a^2 - 9b^2 = (5a + 3b)(5a - 3b)$$
(One factor is the sum of the square roots; the other factor is the difference between the square roots.)

- You can use 'square minus a square' in arithmetic, e.g. without using a calculator evaluate $225^2 - 215^2$.

  $$225^2 - 215^2 = (225 + 215)(225 - 215) = 440 \times 10 = 4400$$

- 'Square minus a square' is sometimes useful when simplifying expressions like this one:

  $$\frac{x^2 + 5x + 6}{x^2 - 9}$$

  $$\frac{x^2 + 5x + 6}{x^2 - 9} = \frac{(x + 2)(x + 3)}{(x + 3)(x - 3)}$$
  (factorise the numerator and the denominator)

  $$= \frac{(x + 2)}{(x - 3)}$$
  (after cancelling)

Question Bank 35

1 Match each expression with its square root.

   a $25x^2$ ☐   **b** $25x^2y^2$ ☐   **c** $225x^2y^2$ ☐   **d** $5x^2y^2$ ☐

   (i) $15xy$ (ii) $5xy$ (iii) $5x$ (iv) $5\sqrt{xy}$

2 Which of these expressions is 'a square minus a square'?

   a $c^2 - 2cd + d^2$ ☐

   b $25x^2y - 16xy^2$ ☐

   c $x^2 - \dfrac{y^2}{4}$ ☐

   d $a^2 - 8$ ☐

3 Factorise $24a^3 - 6ab^2$.

4 Simplify $\dfrac{p^2 - 5p + 4}{p^2 - 16}$

5 Without using a calculator, find $55^2 - 44^2$.

GRADE BOOSTER

'Square minus a square' is really useful. It's worth learning.

Inequalities 1

An inequality tells you about two things that aren't equal.

■ **Showing inequalities on the number line**

$x < 4$ means x is **less than** 4. (The open circle shows that x *cannot be equal* to 4.)

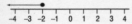

$x \leq -2$ means x is **less than or equal to** -2. (The closed circle shows that x *can be equal to* -2.)

```
—•——————————
-4 -3 -2 -1  0  1  2  3  4
```

$n > -4$ means n is **greater than** -4.

```
———○————————————→
-5 -4 -3 -2 -1  0  1  2  3
```

$n \geq -3$ means n is **greater than or equal to** -3.

```
————•———————————→
-5 -4 -3 -2 -1  0  1  2  3
```

$3 < a < 7$ means a is greater than 3 and less than 7.

```
————————○———————○—
-1  0  1  2  3  4  5  6  7
```

$-2 \leq b \leq 5$ means b is greater than or equal to -2 and less than or equal to 5.

```
——•—————————————•—
-3 -2 -1  0  1  2  3  4  5
```

$3 < f \leq 7$ means f is greater than 3 and less than or equal to 7.

```
————————○—————————•
-1  0  1  2  3  4  5  6  7
```

■ You solve inequalities in the same way as you solve equations.

Solve these inequalities and illustrate the solutions on a number line.

a $2(x - 3) \leq 12$

$2x - 6 \leq 12$
(multiply out the brackets)

$2x \leq 18$ (add 6 to both sides)

$x \leq 9$ (divide both sides by 2)

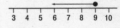

b $7 - 2n < 3 + n$

$7 - 3 < n + 2n$ (collect like terms)

$4 < 3n$

$3n > 4$ (change over sides)

$n > \frac{4}{3}$

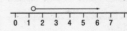

Question Bank 36

1 Write down the inequalities shown below.

a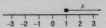

b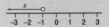

2 Which of the following inequalities is shown on the number line?

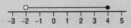

  a $-2 < f < 4$ ☐   **c** $-2 \leq f \leq 4$ ☐

  b $-2 > f < 4$ ☐   **d** $-2 < f \leq 4$ ☐

3 Solve the inequality $3n - 5 > 7$.

4 The solution to the inequality $4c - 9 \leq c + 3$ is:

  a $c \leq 4$ ☐   **c** $c < 4$ ☐

  b $c \leq -2$ ☐   **d** $c \geq 2$ ☐

5 If $-2 \leq x < 5$ and x is an integer, write down the possible values of x.

GRADE BOOSTER

Avoid dividing an inequality by a negative number. If you do, you have to remember to reverse the sign, e.g. $3 > -1$ but $-3 < 1$.

Inequalities 2

A picture is worth a thousand words! Sometimes it's useful to show inequalities on a graph. Here's how.

Show these inequalities on a graph.

a $-1 < x \le 3$

b $y < x + 3$

a

b

(Shade the unwanted region. A full line is part of the region; a dashed line is not.)

Describe the unshaded regions in these diagrams:

a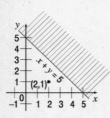

b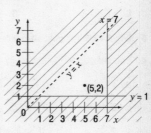

(Use a trial point to check your answer.)

a $x + y \le 5$

b $x > y, x \le 7, y \ge 1$

■ You can show the solution of several inequalities on a graph.

Show the region that satisfies the inequalities $x + y < 6$, $x \ge -1$, $y > 2$.

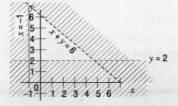

Question Bank 37

1. Describe the unshaded region.

2. Choose the correct answer from the options below.

The unshaded region is:

a $2 < y < 4$ ☐

b $2 \leq y \leq 4$ ☐

c $2 \leq y < 4$ ☐

d $2 < y \leq 4$ ☐

3. Choose the correct answer from the options below.

The boundaries of the unshaded region are:

a $y = x - 3, x = y, x = 3$ ☐

b $x = 3, x + y = 3, y = x + 3$ ☐

c $y = 3, x = 3, x = y + 3$ ☐

d $x = 6, x + y = 6, y = x + 3$ ☐

4. Which of these points is in the unshaded region?

a $(1, 2)$ ☐

b $(5, 5)$ ☐

c $(1, 5)$ ☐

d $(2, 1)$ ☐

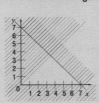

Trial and improvement

Some equations don't have exact solutions and can't be solved by a recognised method. But you can find a solution, accurate to several decimal places, using trial and improvement. Each trial brings you closer to the answer. All you need is a calculator!

This is how you do it.

Solve the equation $x^3 + x = 50$, correct to 2 d.p.

$3^3 + 3 = 30$ and $4^3 + 4 = 68$, so the solution is between 3 and 4.
(Estimate the solution to 1 s.f.)

Try $x = 3.5$ (improve on your estimate)

   $3.5^3 + 3.5 = 46.375$ too small

Try $x = 3.6$

   $3.6^3 + 3.6 = 50.256$ too big

The solution is between 3.5 and 3.6 – probably nearer 3.6 as this gives a solution quite close to 50.

Try $x = 3.58$ (improve again)

   $3.58^3 + 3.58 = 49.462712$ too small

Try $x = 3.59$

   $3.59^3 + 3.59 = 49.858279$ too small

Try 3.595   (You must work to 3 d.p. so that you can give the answer correct to 2 d.p.)

   $3.595^3 + 3.595 = 50.05687$ too big

The solution is between 3.59 and 3.595.

$x = 3.59$ to 2 d.p.

Question Bank 38

1 Between which two integers is the solution of the equation $2x^2 + x = 25$?

2 The solution of the equation $x^2 + \dfrac{10}{x} = 20$ lies between 4 and 5.

Which of these values of x should you try first?

a 4.1 ☐

b 4.9 ☐

c 4.25 ☐

d 4.5 ☐

3 To solve the equation $x^2 - 2x = 300$, what value of x should be tried first?

4 Without using the power key or the square root key on your calculator, find the square root of 60 to 2 s.f.

5 The solution to the equation $x^3 + 2x = 20$ lies between which two integers?

GRADE BOOSTER

It's quite easy to get full marks in a trial and improvement question. Remember to work to one more decimal place than is required in the answer so that you can round to the degree of accuracy asked for.

Real-life graphs

> *A favourite topic in exams is the change in water level as a container is filled, so get plenty of practice on that.*

Conversion graphs, like the one below, are always straight lines.

Use the graph to:

a convert to euros   (i) £55   (ii) £100

b convert to pounds   (i) €40   (ii) €140

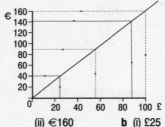

a   (i) €90   (ii) €160   **b** (i) £25   (ii) £88

Other types of real-life graphs are those showing fluctuations in:

■ temperature   ■ prices   ■ heart rate

and graphs showing how the depth of water in a container changes as it fills or empties.

The graph below shows how the depth of water changes as the swimming pool is filled.

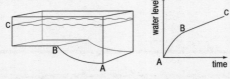

The pool fills most quickly at first and gradually more slowly, and at B the rate becomes constant.

The steep part of the graph shows when the pool is filling fastest. The curved part of the graph, AB, shows that the rate of change of depth is slowing down and the straight part of the graph, BC, shows that the depth is increasing at a constant rate.

Question Bank 39

1 Use this graph to convert:

   a 25°C to °F

   b 50°F to °C.

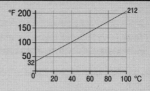

2 The graph shows the number of cars in a concert hall car park from 6 p.m. to 11 p.m. when the car park closed.

a How many cars does the car park hold?

b What time did the concert finish?

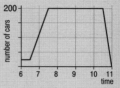

3 The graph shows fluctuations in the price of a company's shares over 6 months. Estimate the highest and lowest prices.

4 Water is poured at a constant rate into the containers A, B and C. Match the graphs with the containers.

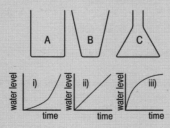

Distance-time graphs

The graph shows Alice's journey from Ayton to Ceeford via Beeham.

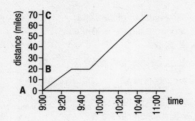

From the graph you can find journey times, distances and speeds.

The distance from Ayton to Beeham is 20 miles and from Beeham to Ceeford is 50 miles.

The time from Ayton to Beeham is 30 minutes. Alice stops for 20 minutes at Beeham and her journey to Ceeford takes 1 hour.

The gradient of the graph = distance ÷ time = speed.

Speed from Ayton to Beeham = $20 \div \frac{1}{2}$

$\quad$ = 40 m.p.h. $\qquad$ (Take care that the time is in the right units, in this example, hours.)

Speed from Beeham to Ceeford = $50 \div 1 = 50$ mph

Average speed for whole journey (including stop)

$$= 70 \div 1\frac{5}{6} = 38 \text{ mph to 2 s.f.}$$

Average speed for whole journey (excluding stop)

$$= 70 \div 1\frac{1}{2} = 47 \text{ mph to 2 s.f.}$$

Question Bank 40

The graph shows Sam's journey to the hypermarket. On the way home, Sam stopped to buy petrol and check his tyre pressures.

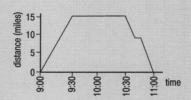

1 What time did Sam arrive at the hypermarket?

2 How far is the hypermarket from Sam's home?

3 What was his average speed on the way to the hypermarket?

4 How long did Sam spend at the hypermarket?

5 How long did he spend at the garage?

GRADE BOOSTER

Quantity represented by gradient =
(quantity on vertical axis) ÷ (quantity on horizontal axis).

Speed-time graphs

Velocity is speed in a stated direction.

The graph shows the first 20 seconds of Adam's journey.

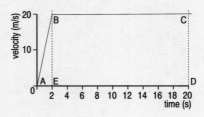

From the graph you can find the acceleration, the total distance travelled and the average speed for the whole journey.

The gradient of the graph = $\dfrac{\text{velocity (speed)}}{\text{time}}$ = acceleration.

The area under the graph (speed × time) = distance travelled.

Acceleration from A to B = gradient of AB = $20 \div 2 = 10\,\text{m/s}^2$

The horizontal line BC shows that Adam was travelling at a steady speed for the remaining 18 seconds.

Total distance travelled
= area of ABE + area of BCDE = $\frac{1}{2} \times 2 \times 20 + 18 \times 20 = 380\,\text{m}$

Average speed = $\dfrac{\text{total distance}}{\text{total time}}$

$$= \frac{380}{20} = 19\,\text{m/s}$$

Question Bank 41

The velocity-time graph shows Bob approaching traffic lights at red. The lights then change to green and he accelerates.

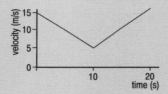

1 For how long was Bob slowing down?

2 What was Bob's acceleration at first (negative because he is slowing down)?

3 What was his speed at the time when the lights changed?

4 How long did he take to accelerate back to his original speed?

5 What was the total distance Bob travelled in the 20 seconds?

GRADE BOOSTER

**Quantity represented by area under a graph =
quantity on vertical axis × quantity on horizontal axis.**

Quadratic equations 1

> A quadratic equation contains an x^2-term, e.g. $x^2 + 5x + 6 = 0$. Usually there are two solutions. If you can factorise the equation, you can solve it.

Examples

Solve the equations:

a $x^2 + 5x + 6 = 0$

b $y^2 - 9y - 10 = 0$

c $c^2 - 4 = 0$

a $x^2 + 5x + 6 = 0$ (factorise)

    $(x + 3)(x + 2) = 0$

Since the factors have a product of zero, one of the factors must be equal to zero.

Either $x + 3 = 0$ or $x + 2 = 0$

so $x = -3$ or $x = -2$

Check in the original equation:

$(-3)^2 + 5(-3) + 6 = 0$ and $(-2)^2 + 5(-2) + 6 = 0$

b $y^2 - 9y - 10 = 0$

    $(y - 10)(y + 1) = 0$

    Either $y - 10 = 0$ or $y + 1 = 0$

    So $y = 10$ or $y = -1$ (Remember to check your answers.)

c $c^2 - 4 = 0$ (This is still a quadratic equation because it has a c^2-term.)

    $(c + 2)(c - 2) = 0$ (Factors of 'a square minus a square'.)

    Either $c + 2 = 0$ or $c - 2 = 0$

    So $c = -2$ or $c = 2$ (Check!)

Question Bank 42

1 Factorise $x^2 + 4x + 3$.

2 The factors of $a^2 - 9a + 18 = 0$ are:

   a $(a - 9)(a - 2)$ ☐

   b $(a - 6)(a - 3)$ ☐

   c $(a + 6)(a + 3)$ ☐

   d $(a - 2)(a - 7)$ ☐

3 If $(f + 4)(2f - 3) = 0$, then f equals:

   a -4 or $+3$ ☐

   b $+4$ or -3 ☐

   c -4 or $+1\frac{1}{2}$ ☐

   d 4 or $\frac{2}{3}$ ☐

4 Solve the equation $2x^2 - 4x = 0$. (One of the factors is $2x$.)

5 Solve the equation $x^2 + 7x + 10 = 0$.

GRADE BOOSTER

The key to solving quadratic equations lies in the fact that the product of the two factors is zero. This means you can say one or other of the factors must be zero and this leads to the two solutions.

Quadratic equations 2

> *The more you practise solving quadratic equations, the easier they become.*

■ Sometimes you have to simplify the equation before you can factorise it.

Examples

Solve the equations:

a $2a^2 + 4a - 30 = 0$

b $r(r + 1) = 8 - r = 0$

a $2a^2 + 4a - 30 = 0$ (Divide each side of the equation by 2.)

    $a^2 + 2a - 15 = 0$

    $(a + 5)(a - 3) = 0$

    Either $a + 5 = 0$ or $a - 3 = 0$

    So $a = -5$ or $a = 3$ (Check the answer.)

b $r(r + 1) = 8 - r$ (Simplify the equation first.)

    $r^2 + r - 8 + r = 0$

    $r^2 + 2r - 8 = 0$

    $(r + 4)(r - 2) = 0$

    Either $r + 4 = 0$ or $r - 2 = 0$

    So $r = -4$ or $r = 2$ (Check.)

■ Some quadratic equations don't have a number at the end.

Example

Solve the equation $p^2 - 4p = 0$.

$p^2 - 4p = 0$

$p(p - 4) = 0$

Either $p = 0$ or $p - 4 = 0$

So $p = 0$ or $p = 4$ (Check.)

Question Bank 43

1 Simplify the equation $x(x + 6) = -5x - 12$.

2 True or false?

   The solutions to the equation $b^2 - 5 = 0$, are $b = 5$ or $b - 5$.

3 Factorise $3c^2 + 15c - 18$.

4 The factors of the quadratic equation $2b(b + 1) = 10 - 6b$ are:

   a $(b + 1)(b - 5)$ ☐

   b $2(b + 5)(b - 1)$ ☐

   c $2(b + 1)(b - 5)$ ☐

   d $(b + 5)(b - 1)$ ☐

GRADE BOOSTER

Practise recognising the different types of quadratics. If there's an x^2-term (and no higher term) then it's a quadratic.

Quadratic graphs

The good news about quadratic graphs is that you know what they look like and it's easy to check your answer by substituting in the original equation. So you can get full marks!

The graph of a quadratic (x^2) function is a **parabola**, a U–shaped curve.

Example

Draw the graph of $y = x^2 + x - 4$ and use it to solve the equation $x^2 + x - 4 = 0$.

First draw up a table of values.

x	–3	–2	–1	0	1	2
x^2	9	4	1	0	1	4
x	–3	–2	–1	0	1	2
–4	–4	–4	–4	–4	–4	–4
y	2	–2	–4	–4	–2	2

Draw the axes; scale them carefully and plot the points. Join the points with a smooth curve.

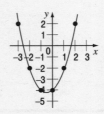

The solution of the equation $x^2 + x - 4 = 0$ is where the graph crosses the x-axis, at $x = -2.6$ and $x = 1.6$ approximately.

Check: when $x = -2.6$, $y = -2.6^2 - 2.6 - 4 = 0.16$

when $x = 1.6$, $y = 1.6^2 + 1.6 - 4 = 0.16$

This is a reasonable degree of accuracy for an answer read from a graph.

Question Bank 44

1 Complete this table for the function $y = x^2 - x - 3$.

x	−2	−1	0	1	2	3
x^2	4	1	0	1	4	9
$-x$	2	1	0	−1	−2	−3
-3	−3	−3	−3	−3	−3	−3
y						

2 Use the graph to write down approximate solutions to the equation $x^2 - 2x - 4 = 0$.

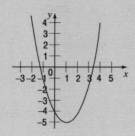

3 If $y = x^2 + 3x - 3$, what is the value of y when $x = 1$?

4 Factorise the equation $x^2 + 4x + 3 = 0$.

5 Use your answer to question 4 to write down the coordinates of the points where the graph of $y = x^2 + 4x + 3$ crosses the x-axis.

GRADE BOOSTER

It's worth checking all along the way.
Check: (1) you have calculated points correctly, (2) you have marked the scales on the axes correctly, (3) you have plotted the points correctly, and (4) the solutions give an answer close to zero when you substitute them in the equation.

Cubic and reciprocal graphs

Get familiar with the basic shapes of cubic and reciprocal graphs. A cubic graph goes round the bend twice and a reciprocal graph has two arms.

Plot these graphs in the usual way by drawing up a table of values and choosing suitable scales for the axes.

■ This is the graph of a typical **cubic** function, $y = x^3 - 2x$.

x	−2	−1	−0.5	0	0.5	1	2
x^3	−8	−1	−0.125	0	0.125	1	8
$-2x$	4	2	1	0	−1	−2	−4
y	−4	1	0.875	0	−0.875	−1	4

The graph of $y = -x^3 + 2x$ is a reflection of this graph in the x-axis.

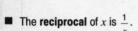

■ The **reciprocal** of x is $\dfrac{1}{x}$.

Here is a graph of the reciprocal function $y = \dfrac{1}{x}$.

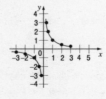

x	−3	−2	−1	$-\dfrac{1}{2}$	$\dfrac{1}{2}$	1	2	3
$y = \dfrac{1}{x}$	$-\dfrac{1}{3}$	$-\dfrac{1}{2}$	−1	−2	2	1	$\dfrac{1}{2}$	$\dfrac{1}{3}$

Notice that you cannot work out a y-value for $x = 0$.

Question Bank 45

1 Match the functions with the graphs.

a $y = x^2 + 3x - 4$

c $y = -x^2 + 2$

b $y = \frac{1}{x}$

d $y = x^3 - x + 2$

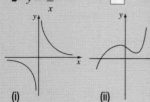 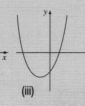 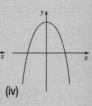

(i)   (ii)   (iii)   (iv)

2 Fill in the missing values in the table for the function $y = \frac{12}{x}$.

x	-12	-6	-4	-3	-2	-1	1	2	3	4	6	12
$y = \frac{12}{x}$	-1			-4			12				2	

3 This is the graph of $y = x^3$.
How could you change it into
the graph of $y = -x^3$?

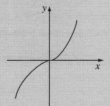

Graphs of simple loci

*Take a look at the examples here. A **locus** is the path a point can take when it moves according to a certain rule.*

■ If two points are on the same horizontal line on a graph, the locus of a point that moves so that it is equidistant from them is a vertical line.

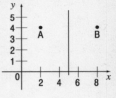

The locus of a point that is equidistant from A and B is the line $x = 5$.

(5 is the mean of the x-coordinates.)

■ If the two points are on a vertical line, the locus is a horizontal line.

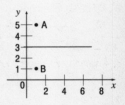

The locus of a point that is equidistant from A and B is $y = 3$.

(3 is the mean of the y-coordinates.)

■ The locus of points equidistant from both axes is a pair of lines, $y = x$ and $y = -x$. The lines are the bisectors of the angles between the axes.

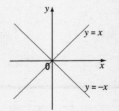

■ Points equidistant from the origin lie on a circle.

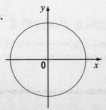

Question Bank 46

1 The equation of the locus of points equidistant from (1, 4) and (1, 7) is:

   a $x = 1$ ☐

   b $y = 5.5$ ☐

   c $x = 5.5$ ☐

   d $y = 1$ ☐

2 Which of these is the locus of points equidistant from the origin?

   a   **b**

3 Match the equations to the diagrams.

   a   **b**   **c**

   (i) $y = -1$ (ii) $y = x$ (iii) $x = -1$

GRADE BOOSTER

Learn these basic types and you should be able to get full marks on a locus question.

Direct proportion

This topic is really quite straightforward. Take a look at the examples on this page.

■ If you walk at a steady speed, the distance, d, you cover is directly proportional to the time, t, you take. This is written as

$d \propto t$

You can replace the $\propto$ sign with $= k$.

$d = kt$

It's easy to work out the value of k.

At 3 mph you cover 3 miles in 1 hour, 6 miles in 2 hours and so on.

Put the numbers in a table.

Time	$\frac{1}{2}$	1	$1\frac{1}{2}$	2
Distance	$1\frac{1}{2}$	3	$4\frac{1}{2}$	6

So $d = 3t$

■ The shadow of a building is in direct proportion to its height. At 12 noon the shadow of a building 15 m high is 8 m long. How high is a building with an 11 m shadow?

$l \propto h$ (write the relationship with a $\propto$ sign)

$l = kh$ (replace the $\propto$ sign with $k =$)

$8 = 15k$ (substitute given values in equation)

$k = \frac{8}{15}$ (find k)

The equation is $l = \frac{8}{15}h$

$11 = \frac{8}{15} \times h$ (use equation to find unknown height)

$h = \frac{15 \times 11}{8}$

$= 21$ m to 2 s.f.

Question Bank 47

1 y is directly proportional to x. Fill in the missing values in the table.

x	2	5	7	
y			17.5	25

2 The volume, V, of a ball is directly proportional to the cube of its radius, r.

If the volume of a ball is $36\,cm^3$ and its radius is $3\,cm$, the value of k in the equation $V = kr^3$ is:

a 12 ☐   **c** $\frac{3}{2}$ ☐

b 4 ☐   **d** $\frac{4}{3}$ ☐

3 In town, my car goes 12 miles on 2 litres of petrol. How many miles can I drive in town on 17 litres?

a 102 ☐   **c** 1.4 ☐

b 204 ☐   **d** 408 ☐

4 On a map a lake is 1.5 cm long. The true length of the lake is 0.75 km.

On the same map, how long would a road 3.5 km long appear?

a 17.5 cm ☐   **c** 7 cm ☐

b 0.7 cm ☐   **d** 1.75 cm ☐

5 $2\frac{1}{2}$ kg of potatoes cost 85p. How much (to the nearest penny) for 12 kg?

GRADE BOOSTER

If two things are in direct proportion, when one goes up so does the other. If one goes down, so does the other.

Section 3 Shape, Space & Measures

Angles 1

Learn these key definitions and you should be able to get full marks on angle questions.

- An **acute** angle is less than 90°.

- A **right** angle is 90°.

- An **obtuse** angle is more than 90° and less than 180°.

- A **reflex** angle is more than 180° and less than 360°.

- Angles on a straight line add up to 180°. $a + b = 180°$

- Angles at a point add up to 360°. $a + b + c + d = 360°$

- **Perpendicular** lines are at 90° to each other.

- When two lines cross they make two pairs of equal angles called **vertically opposite** angles.

Question Bank 48

1 Pick out the obtuse angles.

  a 56° ☐

  b 179° ☐

  c 85° ☐

  d 325° ☐

  e 98° ☐

2 Angle *a* is:

  a 108° ☐

  b 54° ☐

  c 72° ☐

  d 216° ☐

3 What size is angle *x*?

4 Angle *x* is:

  a 30° ☐

  b 70° ☐

  c 35° ☐

  d 60° ☐

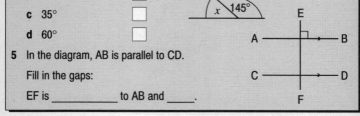

5 In the diagram, AB is parallel to CD.

  Fill in the gaps:

  EF is _____ to AB and _____.

GRADE BOOSTER

When you're finding an angle, you often need to find some of the other angles in the diagram first.

Angles 2

Whenever you see parallel lines there are some equal angles lurking about!

- **Parallel** lines are always the same distance apart – like railway lines.

A line crossing parallel lines makes several pairs of equal angles. The arrows show you the parallel lines.

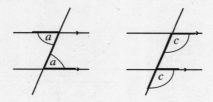

The angles marked a are **alternate angles** (or **Z** angles). The angles marked c are **corresponding angles** (or **F** angles).

- Alternate angles are equal; so are correspondng angles.

- The **angle sum** of a triangle is **180°**.

$$a + b + c = 180°$$

- The **exterior** (outside) angle of a triangle is equal to the sum of the two **interior** (inside) angles at the other two vertices.

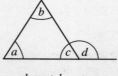

$$d = a + b$$

Question Bank 49

1 What size is angle x?

2 Angle a is:

    a 93°   ☐

    b 97°   ☐

    c 87°   ☐

    d 83°   ☐

3 Angle x is:

    a 30°   ☐

    b 70°   ☐

    c 40°   ☐

    d 60°   ☐

4 The lines AB and CD are parallel. What sizes are angles x and y?

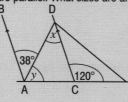

GRADE BOOSTER

Practise finding F angles and Z angles.

Triangles and quadrilaterals

> *Once you've looked at this page, try writing out the key facts to see if you remember them.*

■ An **equilateral** triangle has three equal sides and three equal angles.

■ An **isosceles** triangle has two equal sides and two equal angles.

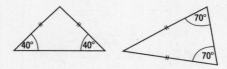

■ In a **scalene** triangle there are no equal sides or angles.

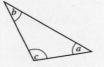

■ A **quadrilateral** has four sides. You can split a quadrilateral into two triangles.

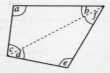

$a + b + c = 180°$ and $d + e + f = 180°$;
so angle sum of a quadrilateral = 360°.

Question Bank 50

1 What sort of triangle is BCD?

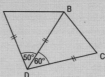

2 Angle *r* is:

   a 50° ☐

   b 70° ☐

   c 20° ☐

   d 30° ☐

3

a	b	c	d
133° ?	76° ? 80°	87° 95° ?	108° 118° ? 77°

Match the angles with the diagrams.

(i) 114°   (ii) 57°   (iii) 47°   (iv) 88°

4 What size is angle *p*?

GRADE BOOSTER

Quadrilaterals crop up all over the place. Whatever sort they are (parallelograms, rhombuses, kites, trapeziums, etc.), their angle sum is 360°.

Quadrilaterals

Take a look at the properties of different types of quadrilaterals.

- **Square**
  four equal sides
  all angles 90°
  opposite sides parallel
  equal diagonals bisect at right angles
  four lines of symmetry
  rotational symmetry order 4

- **Rectangle**
  opposite sides equal and parallel
  all angles 90°
  equal diagonals bisect each other
  two lines of symmetry
  rotational symmetry order 2

- **Parallelogram**
  opposite sides parallel and equal
  opposite angles equal
  diagonals bisect each other
  no lines of symmetry
  rotational symmetry order 2

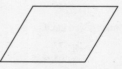

- **Rhombus**
  four equal sides
  opposite sides parallel
  opposite angles equal
  diagonals bisect at right angles
  two lines of symmetry
  rotational symmetry order 2

- **Kite**
  two pairs of adjacent (joining) sides equal
  diagonals cross at right angles
  one line of symmetry

- **Trapezium**
  one pair of parallel sides

Question Bank 51

1   What are the names of these quadrilaterals?

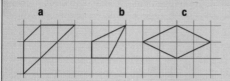

   a   b   c

2   Choose the correct option below.

   A quadrilateral has four equal sides, and its opposite sides are parallel.
   The quadrilateral could be a:

   (i)   square   a   (i) and (ii) only   ☐

   (ii) parallelogram   b   (i) and (iii) only   ☐

   (iii) rhombus   c   any of these   ☐

   (iv) kite   d   (i), (ii) and (ii) only ☐

3   What size is angle a?

4   ABCD is a square.
   What are the coordinates of D?

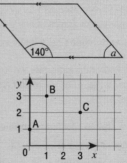

Polygons

Polygons are many-sided flat shapes. Let's start by listing the common ones.

Number of sides	Name
3	triangle
4	quadrilateral
5	pentagon
6	hexagon
8	octagon
10	decagon

A polygon with 7 sides has
7 **interior angles** and 7 **exterior angles**.

- Interior angle + exterior angle of
  any polygon = 180°
  (angles on a straight line)
- Sum of exterior angles of any polygon = 360°
- **Regular polygons** have equal sides and equal angles.

- If you know how many sides a regular polygon has, you can work out the exterior angle. Then, once you have the exterior angle, you can find the interior angle.

What size are the interior and exterior angles of a regular pentagon?

Exterior angle = 360° ÷ 5 = 72°

Interior angle = 180° − 72° = 108°

- If you know the size of an interior or exterior angle in a regular polygon, you can work out how many sides it has.

The interior angle of a regular polygon is 140°. How many sides does it have?

Exterior angle = 180° − 140° = 40°

360° ÷ 40° = 9

The polygon has 9 sides.

Question Bank 52

1 The exterior angle of a regular polygon is 30°.
How many sides does it have?

2 The interior angle of a regular polygon is 135°.
What size is the exterior angle?

3 What size is angle *e*?

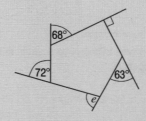

a 72° ☐

b 67° ☐

c 108° ☐

d 113° ☐

4 What size is the interior angle of a regular octagon?

GRADE BOOSTER
You can get a long way if you remember that the sum of the exterior angles is 360°.

Pythagoras' theorem 1

Pythagoras' theorem is about right-angled triangles. It works for any right-angled triangle.

The longest side in a right-angled triangle is opposite the right angle. It is called the **hypotenuse**.

hypotenuse

- Pythagoras' theorem states:

  The square on the hypotenuse is equal to the sum of the squares on the other two sides.

$$a^2 + b^2 = c^2$$

What is the length of the hypotenuse of this triangle?

$$c^2 = 5^2 + 12^2$$
$$= 25 + 144$$
$$= 169$$
$$c = \sqrt{169} = 13$$

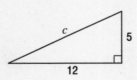

- You can find the length of one of the other sides.

  A ladder 5m long leans against a wall. If the foot of the ladder is 1.5m from the wall, how far up the wall does the ladder reach?

$$5^2 = 1.5^2 + h^2$$
$$h^2 = 5^2 - 1.5^2$$
$$= 25 - 2.25$$
$$= 22.75$$
$$h = \sqrt{22.75} = 4.8\text{m to 2 s.f.}$$

Question Bank 53

1 How long is the hypotenuse of this triangle?

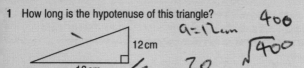

12cm
16cm

(handwritten: a=12cm, 400, √400, /2, 70, √400)

2 A rectangle is 15cm long and 8cm wide. How long is its diagonal?

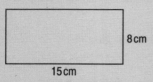

8cm
15cm

3 The length of SR is:

a $\sqrt{5}$ cm

b 3cm

c 5cm

d $\sqrt{29}$ cm

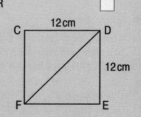

S   2cm   P
1cm
Q
2cm
R

4 CDEF is a square with sides 12cm long.
How long is the diagonal DF,
correct to 2 s.f?

C   12cm   D
12cm
F   E

GRADE BOOSTER

[3, 4, 5] is a *Pythagorean triple* (set of three numbers that are the sides of a right-angled triangle). It's worth remembering some of them: [3, 4, 5]; [5, 12, 13]; [8, 15, 17]; and [7, 24, 25].

Pythagoras' theorem 2

You can use Pythagoras' theorem in isosceles triangles and in 3-D problems too. You'll probably need to add extra lines to the diagram and it's always a good idea to do this, as it helps you to see the problem more clearly.

■ You can use Pythagoras' theorem in an isosceles triangle if you draw in the perpendicular height.

What is the height of an isosceles triangle with base 12 cm and equal sides of length 9 cm?

There are two right-angled triangles, each with sides 6, 9 and h.

$$9^2 = 6^2 + h^2$$
$$h^2 = 9^2 - 6^2$$
$$= 81 - 36$$
$$= 45$$
$$h = \sqrt{45}$$
$$= 6.7 \text{ cm to 2 s.f.}$$

■ 3-D problems

A box is 15 cm long, 5 cm wide and 3 cm high. How long is the longest pencil that will just fit in the box?

The pencil, length l, will fit between two diagonally opposite corners. l is the hypotenuse of a right-angled triangle. To find l, first find d, the base diagonal.

Redraw the triangle containing l and d.
$$d^2 = 15^2 + 5^2$$
$$= 225 + 25$$
$$= 250 \qquad \text{(don't find } d \text{ as you need } d^2 \text{ to get } l\text{)}$$
$$l^2 = d^2 + 3^2$$
$$= 250 + 9$$
$$= 259$$

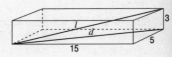

$$l = 16 \text{ cm to 2 s.f.}$$

Question Bank 54

1 A pair of step ladders has sides 2m long. The feet of the ladders are 1m apart.

The top of the steps is h m from the floor.

The equation to work out h is:

a $h^2 = 2^2 - 0.5^2$ ☐

b $h^2 = 2^2 + 50^2$ ☐

c $h^2 = 200^2 + 50^2$ ☐

d $h^2 = 2^2 - 1^2$ ☐

2 The length of OR is:

a 27 ☐   c 45 ☐

b $\sqrt{27}$ ☐   d $\sqrt{45}$ ☐

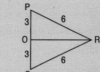

3 How long is the diagonal, AG, of the cube?

4 The mast AB is at the centre of a 20m square. A wire stay joins the top of the mast to a corner of the square. How long is the wire stay?

GRADE BOOSTER

If you draw a clear diagram and show the steps in your working you can get some of the marks, even if you don't manage to finish the question.

Congruent shapes

Congruent is the mathematical word for identical. Two shapes are congruent if they are exactly the same shape and size. They will fit one on top of the other if one of them is reflected, rotated or translated.

These quadrilaterals are congruent.

There are four tests that tell you if two triangles are congruent.

1   Three sides of one triangle are equal to the three sides of the other triangle (**SSS**).

2   Two sides and the angle between them are the same in both triangles (**SAS**).

    Note: The angle *must* be between the two sides in each triangle. If it is not, the triangles are not necessarily congruent.

    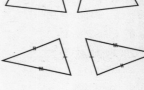

3   Two angles and a side in one triangle are equal to two angles and the corresponding side in the other triangle (**AAS**).

    Note: *Corresponding side* means that the side in question must be in the same relative position in both triangles. If it is not, the triangles are not necessarily congruent.

    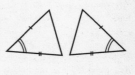

4   Each triangle has a right angle, and the hypotenuse and one other side are the same in both triangles (**RHS**).

Question Bank 55

1 Write down whether each pair of shapes is congruent or not.

a **b** **c** **d**

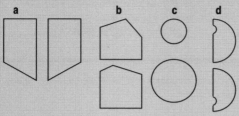

2 Are these triangles congruent?

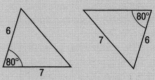

3 AB is equal and parallel to CD. Which test (SSS, SAS, AAS or RHS) tells you that triangles ABX and CDX are congruent?

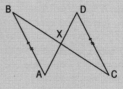

4 Triangle ABC is isosceles. Write down two pairs of congruent triangles and say which test (SSS, SAS, AAS or RHS) applies.

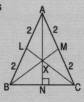

GRADE BOOSTER

Once you've found a pair of congruent triangles, you can find missing angles in a diagram.

Transforming shapes

*Transforming shapes is a big topic in the exam, but it's OK once you realise it's just moving shapes from one place to another. You can transform a shape by **reflecting** (as in a mirror), **rotating** (turning) or **translating** (pushing) it.*

The shape you start with is called the **object** and the shape you finish with is called the **image**.

- In a reflection, rotation or translation the object and the image are **congruent** (same shape and size).

- You describe a **reflection** by naming the **mirror line**, e.g. the y-axis, $x = 3$, etc.

  Triangle B is a reflection of triangle A in the line $x = 1$.

- You describe a **rotation** by naming the **centre**, the **angle** and the **direction** (clockwise or anticlockwise).

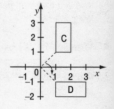

  Rectangle C is rotated 90° clockwise about (0, 0) to rectangle D.

- You describe a **translation** with a **vector**.

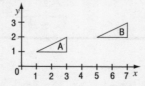

Triangle A is translated to triangle B by the vector $\begin{pmatrix} 4 \\ 1 \end{pmatrix}$

The top number in the vector tells you the number of units across (positive to the right) and the bottom number tells you the number of units up or down (positive up).

Question Bank 56

Triangle A is reflected (image C), rotated (image B) and translated (image D).

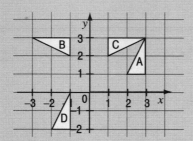

1 What is the equation of the mirror line for the reflection?

2 What is the vector for the translation?

3 What is the centre of the rotation?

4 What is the angle of the rotation?

5 What is the direction of the rotation?

Enlarging shapes

Yet another type of transformation – but this is the last one! You can transform a shape by enlarging it. The image can be bigger or smaller than the object. (It takes a mathematician to call something that makes a shape smaller, an enlargement!)

■ You describe an enlargement by naming the **centre** and the **scale factor**.

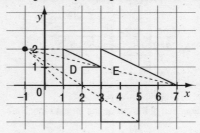

Shape E is an enlargement of shape D with scale factor 2, centre (–1, 2). The lengths in E are 2 × the lengths in D.

■ If the scale factor is greater than 1, the image is bigger than the object.

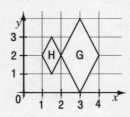

Shape H is an enlargement of shape G with centre (0, 2) and scale factor $\frac{1}{2}$. The lengths in H are $\frac{1}{2}$ × the lengths in G.

■ If the scale factor is a fraction between 0 and 1, the image is smaller than the object.

■ In an enlargement the object and image are **similar** – they are the same shape (all the angles stay the same) but they are not the same size.

Question Bank 57

1 Triangle ABC is enlarged
   with scale factor 3, centre (0, 0).

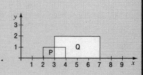

The coordinates of B′,
the image of B, are:

   a (9, 2) ☐   **c** (6, 9) ☐

   b (9, 6) ☐   **d** (3, 6) ☐

2 Shape P is enlarged to shape Q.
   Where is the centre of enlargement?

3 Triangle DEF is enlarged by scale factor $\frac{1}{2}$.
   The area of triangle DEF is $4\,cm^2$.

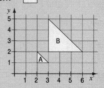

The area of the image is:

   a $4\,cm^2$ ☐   **c** $1\,cm^2$ ☐

   b $2\,cm^2$ ☐   **d** $16\,cm^2$ ☐

4 Triangle A is enlarged to triangle B.
   What is the scale factor of the enlargement?

GRADE BOOSTER

**Remember that an enlargement with scale factor 2 produces a shape
with area 4 × the area of the object.**

Similar shapes

Similarity is one of those topics that pops up in lots of places, so it's worth spending some time getting the hang of it.

■ Two shapes are **similar** if one shape is an enlargement of the other.

Triangles P and Q are similar because they have the same angles.

Circles are all similar to each other and so are squares.

Rectangles E and F are not similar. They have the same angles, but F is not an enlargement of E. The relationship between the long and short sides is not the same.

■ If two shapes are similar, corresponding sides will be in the same ratio.

Triangles LMN and PQR are similar (corresponding sides are in the same ratio).

How long is LM?

$$\frac{LM}{PQ} = \frac{MN}{QR}$$

$$\frac{LM}{2} = \frac{3}{4}$$

$$LM = 1\frac{1}{2}$$

Watch out for similar triangles where one triangle is inside the other.

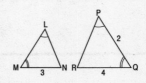

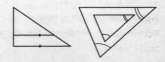

Question Bank 58

1 Which pair of rectangles is similar?

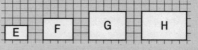

  a E and F ☐   **c** E and G ☐

  b F and G ☐   **d** E and H ☐

2 The triangles are similar. Find x.

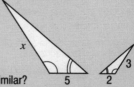

3 P and Q are regular pentagons. Are they similar?

4 I am 1.6 m tall and my brother is 1.8 m. My shadow is 2 m long. How long is my brother's shadow?

  a 2.25 m ☐   **c** 2.2 m ☐

  b 1.8 m ☐   **d** 3 m ☐

5 A photo, 8 cm × 11 cm, is surrounded by a frame 2 cm wide.
Are the frame and the photo similar?

    8

    11

GRADE BOOSTER

The scale factor of the enlargement is the same as the ratio of corresponding sides from the smaller to the larger shape.
For the larger to the smaller shape, the ratio is the reciprocal of the scale factor.

Trigonometry

You can use trigonometry in a right-angled triangle to find a missing side or angle. If you know the three trig ratios, you're off to a head start.

In a right-angled triangle the longest side (opposite the right angle) is the **hypotenuse.** The other two sides are **opposite** and **adjacent** (next to) the angle you are interested in – either because you know its size or because you want to find it.

- The three trig ratios are:

  sin θ = **o**pp/**h**yp **c**os θ = **a**dj/**h**yp **t**an θ = **o**pp/**a**dj

- Use the word **sohcahtoa** to remember which is which.

Find x in this triangle.

hypotenuse = 12 cm   opposite = x

$\sin 42 = \dfrac{x}{12}$

$x = 12 \sin 42 = 8.02956$

$x = 8.0$ cm to 2 s.f.

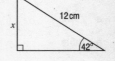

Find θ in this triangle.

hypotenuse = 15   adjacent = 8

$\cos \theta = \dfrac{8}{15} = 0.53333$

$\theta = 57.76 = 58°$ to 2 s.f.

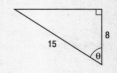

- The angle of **elevation** is the angle you lift your gaze through to look at something above.

- The angle of **depression** is the angle you lower your gaze through to look at something below.

Question Bank 59

1 In this triangle the hypotenuse is:

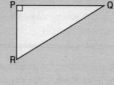

   a PQ

   b QR

   c PR

   d QP

2 Write sin θ as a fraction.

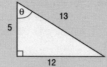

3 Use this diagram to find the value of cos 60°.

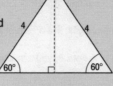

4 Find the length of the side marked x to 2 s.f.

5 Trixie is standing 5 m from the base of a flagpole. The angle of elevation to the top of the pole is 65°. How high is the flagpole?

GRADE BOOSTER

Make sure you know how to use the trig functions on your calculator.

Bearings

Bearings are used in navigation and map reading. The maths is the same as for other topics in this section.

■ Bearings tell you a direction as an angle measured *clockwise* from the North line.

Xavier is walking on a bearing of 080°.

Yolanda is walking on a bearing of 200°.

Zechariah is walking on a bearing of 300° (= 360° − 60°).

■ A bearing always has three digits. Put a zero at the front if necessary.

■ If you know the bearing of A from B, you can work out the bearing of B from A.

The bearing of the ship from the lighthouse is 100°.

The bearing of the lighthouse from the ship is 280°.

■ Bearings crop up in trigonometry problems.

A ship sails 350 km from a port on a bearing of 075° to its destination. How far north and east of the port is the destination?

Start by drawing a diagram.

Distance north = n

Distance east = e

$$\sin 15° = \frac{n}{350}$$

$n = 350 \sin 15° = 90.6$ km to 3 s.f.

$$\cos 15° = \frac{e}{350}$$

$e = 350 \cos 15° = 338$ km to 3 s.f.

Question Bank 60

1 The bearing of the ship from the rocks is:

  a 085° ☐   **c** 265° ☐

  b 275° ☐   **d** 095° ☐

2 Quentin is walking towards Prunella's house on a bearing of 240°.
What bearing should Prunella take if she sets out to meet him?

3 Match these compass directions with the correct bearings.

  a South ☐   **b** NE ☐   **c** NW ☐   **d** SW ☐

  (i) 045°   (ii) 315°   (iii) 180°   (iv) 225°

4 A ship sails 50 km from P on a bearing of 039°.

Its distance north and east of P is:

  a $50\cos 39°$ N, $50\sin 39°$ E ☐   **c** $50\cos 39°$ N, $50\cos 39°$ E ☐

  b $50\sin 39°$ N, $50\sin 39°$ E ☐   **d** $50\cos 51°$ N, $50\sin 51°$ E ☐

GRADE BOOSTER

Always draw the North line at the point from which the bearing is measured.

Circles

You need to know a lot of facts about circles, but they're all easy ones.
Make sure you understand the examples on this page.

■ **Parts of a circle**

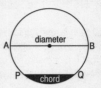

O is the **centre**.

OC is a **radius**.

DC is an **arc**.

The shaded area is a **sector**.

AB is a **diameter**. PQ is a **chord**. The shaded area is a **segment**.

■ The **circumference** is the distance all the way round the edge of the circle.

Use the formula $C = \pi d$ to find the circumference.

$C = \pi \times 5.5\,\text{cm}$

  (use the π button on your calculator)

$= 17\,\text{cm}$ to 2 s.f.

(If you know the radius of the circle,
you double it to get the diameter.)

■ The formula for the area of a circle is $A = \pi r^2$.

$A = \pi \times 2.75^2$ (halve the diameter to get the radius)

$= 24\,\text{cm}^2$ to 2 s.f.

■ The angle at the centre of a circle is 360°.

■ You can construct regular polygons inside circles.
Here's how.

A regular pentagon has five sides.

$360° \div 5 = 72°$

Draw five angles of 72° at the centre of the circle and join up the ends
of the radii.

■ A **cyclic quadrilateral** is a quadrilateral with
all four corners on the circumference of a circle.

$a + c = 180°$ $b + d = 180°$

The opposite angles of a cyclic quadrilateral sum to 180°.

Question Bank 61

1 What size is angle a?

2 Match each circle with
its circumference.
(Do not use a calculator.)

a   **b**   **c**   **d**

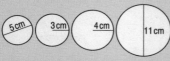

(i) 35 cm   (ii) 25 cm   (iii) 19 cm   (iv) 16 cm

3 This running track has two semi-circular ends of radius 30 m and two
straight parts each 90 m long.

The distance round the track is:

a $\pi \times 30 + 90$ ☐   **c** $\pi \times 60 + 2 \times 90$ ☐

b $\pi \times 60 + 90$ ☐   **d** $\pi \times 120$ ☐

4 True or false?

A circular path 1 m wide surrounds a pond of radius 1 m.

The area of the path is $(4\pi - \pi)$ square metres.

Angles in circles

There are several facts about angles in circles here. Don't be put off by the words – the pictures tell you the story.

A **tangent** is a line that touches a circle.

- A tangent is **perpendicular** to the radius at the point where the tangent touches the circle.

    ∠APO = 90°

- Two tangents from the same point are **equal** in length.

    AB = AC

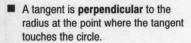

- A line from the centre of a circle perpendicular to a chord bisects the chord.

    PQ = QR

- The angle subtended by an arc at the centre of a circle is twice the angle subtended at any point on the circumference.

    (This means that all the angles subtended on the circumference by the same arc are equal.)

    ∠AOB = 2∠ACB
    ∠AOB = 2∠ADB
    ∠ACB = ∠ADB

- The angle in a semi-circle is a right angle.

    ∠ACB = 90°

Question Bank 62

What size is ∠POT?

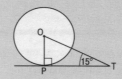

Find angles x and y.

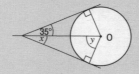

What size is ∠AOB?

Find angle a.

Drawing solids

You can show a 3-D solid in a 2-D drawing. A sketch gives a general impression. Plans and elevations give a more accurate representation.

■ The **plan** is the view of the solid from directly above (the bird's-eye view). Here is the plan of a flight of steps.

■ The **elevation** is the view from the side or the front of the solid. Here are the side and front elevations of the same flight of steps.

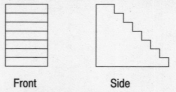

Front   Side

The three views are shown together like this:

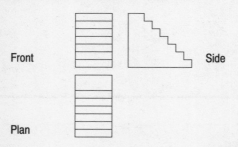

Front   Side

Plan

Here is a plan of a flower pot. Notice that hidden lines are shown by dotted lines.

Question Bank 63

What object is shown in this plan and elevation?

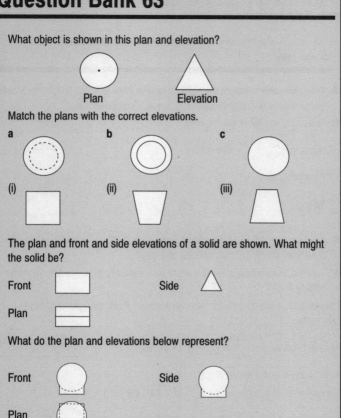

Plan   Elevation

Match the plans with the correct elevations.

a   b   c

(i)   (ii)   (iii)

The plan and front and side elevations of a solid are shown. What might the solid be?

Front   Side

Plan

What do the plan and elevations below represent?

Front   Side

Plan

GRADE BOOSTER

Don't forget that there may be two drawings for the elevation –
a front view and a side view.

Perimeter and area

This topic is straightforward. It's worth memorising the formulae as it speeds up your work.

- The **perimeter** is the distance all round the edge of a flat shape. (In a circle the perimeter is called the circumference – see page 130.)
- These are the formulae for **area**.

Rectangle $A = l \times b$

Parallelogram $A = b \times h$

Triangle $A = \frac{1}{2} b \times h$

- A **prism** is a solid with a uniform cross-section. If you slice the prism, all the slices will be the same shape and size.
- You find the surface area of a prism by finding the area of each face and adding them.

The surface of this triangular prism is made up of two triangles and three rectangles.

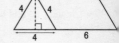

Area of two triangles $= 2 \times (\frac{1}{2} \times 4 \times 4 \sin 60°)$

Area of three rectangles $= 3 \times (4 \times 6)$

Surface area of prism $= 2 \times (\frac{1}{2} \times 4 \times 4 \sin 60°) + 3 \times (4 \times 6)$

$= 86 \, \text{cm}^2$ to 2 s.f.

- A **cylinder** is a prism with a circular cross-section.

The surface area of this cylinder is made up of two circles and a rectangle (think of the label on a can).

Area of two circles $= 2 \times \pi \times r^2 = 2 \times \pi \times 16$

Area of rectangle $= \pi \times d \times h = \pi \times 8 \times 9$

Surface area of cylinder $= 32 \times \pi + 72 \times \pi$

$= 330 \, \text{cm}^2$ to 2 s.f.

Question Bank 64

1

The perimeter of this shape is:

  a 24 ☐   **b** 21 ☐   **c** 25 ☐   **d** 28 ☐

2 Which of these shapes has the longest perimeter?

  a ☐   **b** ☐   **c** ☐

3

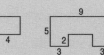

The surface area of this cylinder is:

  a 48π ☐   **b** 78π ☐   **c** 132π ☐   **d** 72π ☐

4 A box is 20 cm long, 15 cm wide and 10 cm high.
What is its surface area?

GRADE BOOSTER

You can put extra measurements on the diagram to help you in your calculations.

Volume

It's worth learning the volume formulae so that you don't waste time searching the formula sheet. You're expected to know the formula for the volume of a cuboid. Volume is measured in cubic units, usually cm^3 or m^3.

■ Volume formulae

Cube $\quad V = a^3$

Cuboid $\quad V = l \times b \times h$

Prism $\quad V =$ area of cross-section $\times$ height (or length)

■ A cubic metre (m^3) is a $100 \times 100 \times 100 = 1\,000\,000\,cm^3$.

To change cm^3 to m^3 divide by $1\,000\,000$ (10^6).

To change m^3 to cm^3 multiply by $1\,000\,000$.

Note: A cubic metre is a large unit!

Examples

a A crate is 60 cm long, 60 cm wide and 70 cm high.

Find its volume in (i) cm^3 (ii) m^3.

$V = 60 \times 60 \times 70 = 252\,000\,cm^3$

Volume in $m^3 = 252\,000 \div 1\,000\,000 = 0.252\,m^3$

b Find the volume of this cylinder in m^3.

$V =$ area of cross-section $\times$ length

$\quad = \pi r^2 \times l$

$\quad = \pi \times 25^2 \times 75 = 147\,262\,cm^3 = 0.15\,m^3$ to 2 s.f.

c Find the volume of this prism.

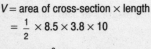

$V =$ area of cross-section $\times$ length

$\quad = \frac{1}{2} \times 8.5 \times 3.8 \times 10$

$\quad = 150\,cm^3$ to 2 s.f.

Question Bank 65

1 What is the volume of this cuboid?

2 A cylinder has a volume of 500 cm³.

Its base radius is 5 cm. Correct to 2 s.f., its height is:

a $\dfrac{500}{5\pi}$ ☐   **c** $\dfrac{500}{100\pi}$ ☐

b $\dfrac{500}{25\pi}$ ☐   **d** $\dfrac{500}{10\pi}$ ☐

3 Match each prism with a formula for its volume.

a   b   c   d

(i) $\dfrac{1}{2}\pi r^2 h$ (ii) $\pi r^2 h$ (iii) x^3 (iv) $\dfrac{1}{2}bh \times l$

4 The end of this unsharpened pencil has an area of 0.5 cm².

The pencil is 15 cm long. What is its volume?

Dimensions

Stephen Hawking thinks there may be 11 dimensions. Luckily you only need 3 in maths!

■ Formulae for **length** have **one dimension**.

The formula for the circumference of a circle is $C = 2\pi r$.

2 and π are numbers. They have no dimensions.

r is a length, the radius of the circle, measured in cm, m, etc.

The perimeter of a rectangle is $2b + 2l$.

Here two lengths are added (not multiplied), so there is still only one dimension.

■ Formulae for **area** have **two dimensions**.

When you find an area you multiply two lengths, e.g. for a triangle $A = \frac{1}{2}bh$.

$\frac{1}{2}$ is a number with no dimension.

b and h are lengths, so the formula has two dimensions.

■ Formulae for **volume** have **three dimensions**.

When you find a volume you multiply three lengths together, e.g. for a cuboid $V = l \times b \times h$

There are three dimensions. This means that it is possible to tell, just by looking at a formula, whether it is a length, area or volume formula.

$\frac{4}{3}\pi r^3$ must be a volume.

$\frac{4}{3}$ and π are just numbers, but

$r \times r \times r$ is three lengths multiplied together so there are three dimensions.

($V = \frac{4}{3}\pi r^3$ is the volume of a sphere.)

$A = \pi r^2 + \pi r h$ is an area (surface area of a cylinder).

In the formula two terms are added together and each term has two dimensions.

Question Bank 66

In these questions a, b, d, h, l and r are lengths.

1 Choose the correct option.

Which of these formulae represent areas?

(i) $\frac{1}{2}(a+b)h$ (ii) a^3 (iii) $\pi r^2 l$ (iv) $\frac{1}{2}ab$

a (i) and (ii) ☐   **c** (i) and (iii) ☐

b (ii) and (iii) ☐   **d** (i) and (iv) ☐

2 How many dimensions does this formula have?

$x = \frac{1}{3}\pi r^2 l + \frac{2}{3}\pi r^3$

3 Select your answer from the options below.

One of these expressions gives the *area* and another gives the *perimeter* of the shape shown in the diagram.

(i) $ab + \frac{\pi a^2}{4}$ (ii) $2a + 2b + \pi a$

(iii) $ab + \pi a^2$ (iv) $\pi a + 2b$

Select the correct expression for:

a the area ☐   **b** the perimeter ☐

4 Does the formula $x = 3(h + l)$ represent a length, an area or a volume?

5 How many dimensions should there be in a formula for each of the following?

a The seating capacity of the Albert Hall

b The perimeter of a running track   **c** The volume of the Earth

d The number of suitcases the singer Alton James takes on a transatlantic flight

---

GRADE BOOSTER

All the terms in a formula must have the same dimensions. It isn't possible to have a formula that represents, say, both area and volume.

Symmetry

We'll start by looking at symmetry in two dimensions and then go on to three-dimensional symmetry.

■ Reflection symmetry in 2-D shapes

The letter **A** has one **line of symmetry**.
If one half of the A is reflected in the line
it makes the other half.

Some shapes have several lines of symmetry.

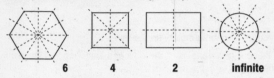

6	4	2	infinite

■ Rotation symmetry in 2-D shapes

The letter **Z** has rotational symmetry order 2.
It has two identical positions when rotated (turned)
about the marked point.

Here are some shapes with rotational symmetry order 2 or higher. (All
shapes have rotational symmetry of order at least 1.)

2	3	2

■ Reflection symmetry in 3-D shapes

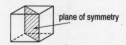

plane of symmetry

A cube has nine planes of symmetry that each cut the cube into two
matching halves. Can you find them all?

Question Bank 67

1 How many lines of symmetry does an equilateral triangle have?

2 What is the order of rotational symmetry of a regular pentagon?

3 How many planes of symmetry does this cuboid have?

a 1 ☐   c 3 ☐

b 2 ☐   d 4 ☐

4 Complete the table below by matching each shape with the correct number of lines of symmetry and order of rotational symmetry.

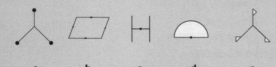

Shape	Lines of symmetry	Order of rotational symmetry
	1	1
	0	3
	0	2
	2	2
	3	3

GRADE BOOSTER

Practise looking for planes of symmetry, as that's the part some students find difficult.

143

Coordinates

The coordinates of a point tell you where it is on a graph. You can work out the length of a line joining two points on a graph and where the midpoint of the line is, from coordinates.

The point (0, 0) on a graph where the axes cross is called the **origin**.

The coordinates of point A (3, 1), tell you it is 3 units along and 1 unit up from the origin (0, 0).

(To help you remember which way round the coordinates go, say '*along* the passage and *up* the stairs'.)

Strictly speaking, lines are infinitely long. AB is a **line segment**.

■ Working out the length of AB

Triangle ABC is right-angled at C.
So you can use Pythagoras' theorem.

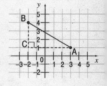

First find the lengths of AC and CB.

C is the point (–2, 1).

The length of AC = difference between x-coordinates of A and C

$= 3 - (-2) = 5$

The length of CB = difference between y-coordinates of B and C

$= 4 - 1 = 3$

$AB^2 = AC^2 + CB^2$

$AB^2 = 5^2 + 3^2 = 34$

$AB = \sqrt{34} = 5.83$

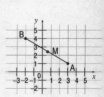

■ Finding the midpoint of AB

Let the midpoint of AB be M.

x-coordinate of M = average of x-coordinates of A and B = $\dfrac{-2+3}{2} = \dfrac{1}{2}$

y-coordinate of M = average of y-coordinates of A and B = $\dfrac{1+4}{2} = 2\dfrac{1}{2}$

The midpoint of AB is $\left(\dfrac{1}{2}, 2\dfrac{1}{2} \right)$

Question Bank 68

Use this diagram to answer the questions.

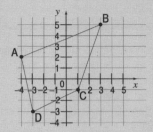

1 How long is DB?

2 True or false?   The midpoint of CD is (–1, –2).

3 Match each line with its length.

   a AB ☐   **b** BC ☐   **c** CD ☐   **d** AD ☐

   (i) $\sqrt{20}$ (ii) $\sqrt{40}$ (iii) $\sqrt{58}$ (iv) $\sqrt{26}$

4 What is the midpoint of BC?

GRADE BOOSTER

Make sure you get x-and y-coordinates the right way round. One
way to remember this is to think that X comes before Y in the
alphabet, so the x-coordinate is the first one.

Loci and constructions

*A **locus** (plural **loci**) is a line or a region made up of all the possible positions of a point that obeys a certain rule. Think of a donkey in a field, tethered to a rope. The donkey can only move inside a circle. The circle is the donkey's locus.*

Suppose a point P always has to be the same distance (equidistant) from two fixed points, A and B.

If you mark some of the possible positions of P, you will see that P has to be on the perpendicular bisector of the line joining A and B. This line is the **locus** of P.

You can construct the locus with a ruler and a pair of compasses.

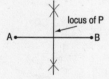

The locus of a point P that is equidistant from two fixed lines is the bisector of the angle between the lines. It is easily constructed with a pair of compasses and a ruler.

locus of P

Another important locus is a circle: the path of points that are equidistant from one fixed point. The fixed point will be the centre of the circle.

You can construct an equilateral triangle using a pair of compasses.

Question Bank 69

1 Point P must be less than 2m from point A and more than 3m from point B.
The locus of P is shown shaded in which of these diagrams?

a   **b**   **c**

2 ABCD is a square field of side 30m. Joe wants to erect a tent so that it is farther from A than it is from B and closer to C than it is to A.

Which diagram shows the area where Joe can erect his tent?

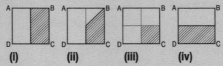

3 Three destroyers, Jupiter, Mars and Thor, are equally spaced in a circle of radius 10km. An enemy submarine is submerged more than 8km from Jupiter and more than 8km from Mars and within 12km of Thor. Which region should you shade on the diagram to show the area in which the submarine might be?

GRADE BOOSTER

Practise using your ruler and compasses to do accurate drawings.

Measures

Here's a straightforward topic to round off this section.

■ When you make a measurement you read a scale. Work out what the large and small divisions stand for before you make the reading.

On this scale the large divisions are 0.1 each and the small divisions are 0.02, so the reading is 0.86.

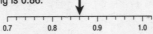

| 0.7 | 0.8 | 0.9 | 1.0 |

■ Metric units have replaced most of the imperial units, but you still need to be able to convert from one to the other.

These approximations are useful. (You will be given them in the exam, but it's worth knowing them anyway.)

5 miles ≈ 8 km	1 kg ≈ 2.2 pounds
1 inch ≈ 2.5 cm	1 litre ≈ $1\frac{3}{4}$ pints
1 metre ≈ 39 inches	4.5 litres ≈ 1 gallon

Examples

a Change 50 km to miles.   8 km ≈ 5 miles

$1\text{km} \approx \frac{5}{8}$ mile   (the unitary method)

$50\text{km} \approx 50 \times \frac{5}{8}$ ≈ 31 miles to 2 s.f.

b Change a speed of 30 mph to km/h.

5 miles ≈ 8 km   1 mile ≈ $\frac{8}{5}$ km

$30 \text{ miles} \approx 30 \times \frac{8}{5}$ ≈ 50 km/h to 1 s.f.

You might be asked to change a speed in km/h to a speed in m/s or vice versa.

What is 6 m/s in km/h?

6 m in 1 s = 6 × 60 × 60 m in 1 h $= \frac{6 \times 60 \times 60}{1000}$ km in 1 h

= 21.6 km in 1 h   = 20 km/h to 1 s.f.

148

Question Bank 70

1 What is the reading on this scale?

2 Roughly how many litres are there in 8 gallons?

3 A litre is 1000 cc (cubic centimetres, or cm^3).
The number of litres in 1 cubic metre is:

a 1 000 000 ☐   **c** 1000 ☐

b 100 ☐   **d** 10 ☐

4 There are 3 feet in 1 yard and 1760 yards in 1 mile. The correct calculation to convert a speed of 88 feet per second to m.p.h. is:

a $\dfrac{88 \times 3 \times 1760}{60 \times 60}$ ☐   **c** $\dfrac{1760 \times 3}{88 \times 60}$ ☐

b $\dfrac{88 \times 60}{1760 \times 3}$ ☐   **d** $\dfrac{88 \times 60 \times 60}{3 \times 1760}$ ☐

5 Which is better value, 50p per pound or 105p per kilo?

Selecting data

> *Some questions can be answered using statistics, e.g. 'Is the Puritan Party likely to win the next General Election?' Others, such as, 'Was Maria Callas a better singer than Elvis Presley?', cannot. You could survey people's voting intentions and make an estimate of the PP's chances. Callas and Presley had different styles of singing and probably appeal to different groups of people.*

■ To carry out a statistical survey you have to decide what questions to ask.

Questions that can be answered 'yes' or 'no' are suitable. The answers are easy to analyse.

Questions with tick boxes are also suitable.

The question 'Do you take your holidays in Britain or abroad?' is unsuitable because it is too vague.

■ You have to do your best to make sure that the data you collect are not **biased**.

If you are doing a traffic survey, you need data for various times of day and different days of the week.

Questions such as: 'The *Daily Rag* says that teenagers should get more pocket money. Do you think you should get more pocket money?' are not suitable. This is a leading question – it leads the person answering to say 'Yes'.

■ If the group you are surveying is small, you can ask everyone in it. If not, you have to ask a representative **sample**. You have to choose the sample so that it is not biased.

Suppose you want to know what the students at your school think of school dinners. Your sample should include some pupils from each year group and some who bring sandwiches.

Question Bank 71

1 Which of these questions are suitable for a questionnaire?

   a How much pocket money do you get? Tick one box.

   under £5 ☐   £5–£10 ☐   over £10 ☐

   b Students who have plenty of sleep tend to do better in exams. Do you intend to go to bed early when you are taking your GCSEs?

   c Is Madonna a better singer than Angela Gheorghiu (an opera singer)?

   d Where will you take your next holiday? Tick one box.

   Britain ☐   Europe ☐   USA ☐   Caribbean ☐

2 Which of these might give biased data?

   a Finding absentee rates at a factory by looking at the attendance every Friday for 5 weeks. ☐

   b Asking motorists at a petrol station if the duty on petrol is too high. ☐

   c Finding out how students travel to school by asking every tenth person on the school register. ☐

   d Doing a survey of which breakfast cereal children prefer in a week when Wheety Bangs are giving away Harry Potter souvenirs. ☐

GRADE BOOSTER

Vague questions and leading questions are not suitable for use on a questionnaire.

Social statistics

> The government collects, analyses and publishes large amounts of data.
> Some of these data are published as **index numbers**, which are
> updated regularly.

The *General Index of Retail Prices (RPI)*, or the 'cost of living index', was started in 1914. It is published monthly by the Office for National Statistics and tells people how much retail prices (prices in the shops) have increased relative to a certain year. It has to be reset to 100 periodically because of rising prices. It was last reset at 100 in January 1987.

The RPI for September 2001 was 174.6. This means that goods costing a total of £100 in January 1987 would cost £174.60 in September 2001.

The RPI is used by managers and employee representatives for wage and salary negotiations.

Here is the RPI for January 2000–September 2001.

The **inflation** rate (the rate at which prices are increasing) is given in the third column. A rate of 2.0% means that prices now are 2.0% higher than they were a year ago. To calculate the rate of inflation in September 2001 you do this calculation:

Year	Month	Index	Inflation rate ++ %
2000	January	166.6	2.0
	February	167.5	2.3
	March	168.4	2.6
	April	170.1	3.0
	May	170.7	3.1
	June	171.1	3.3
	July	170.5	3.3
	August	170.5	3.0
	September	171.7	3.3
	October	171.6	3.1
	November	172.1	3.2
	December	172.2	2.9
2001	January	171.1	2.7
	February	172.0	2.7
	March	172.2	2.3
	April	173.1	1.8
	May	174.2	2.1
	June	174.4	1.9
	July	173.3	1.6
	August	174.0	2.1
	September	174.6	1.7
++percentage change over previous year			Data © HMSO

$$\frac{\text{RPI for Sep 2001} - \text{RPI for Sep 2000}}{\text{RPI for Sep 2000}} \times 100\%$$

$$= \frac{174.6 - 171.7}{171.7} \times 100\% = 1.6889\ldots \qquad = 1.7\% \text{ to 2 s.f.}$$

Question Bank 72

The table shows the RPI from 1987 to 1999. Use it to answer the questions.

Year	Jan	Feb	Mar	Apr	May	June	July	Aug	Sept	Oct	Nov	Dec
1987	100.0	100.4	100.6	101.8	101.9	101.9	101.8	102.1	102.4	102.9	103.4	103.3
1988	103.3	103.7	104.1	105.8	106.2	106.6	106.7	107.9	108.4	109.5	110.0	110.3
1989	111.0	111.8	112.3	114.3	115.0	115.4	115.5	115.8	116.6	117.5	118.5	118.8
1990	119.5	120.2	121.4	125.1	126.2	126.7	126.8	128.1	129.3	130.3	130.0	129.9
1991	130.2	130.9	131.4	133.1	133.5	134.1	133.8	134.1	134.6	135.1	135.6	135.7
1992	135.6	136.3	136.7	138.8	139.3	139.3	138.8	138.9	139.4	139.9	139.7	139.2
1993	137.9	138.8	139.3	140.6	141.1	141.0	140.7	141.3	141.9	141.8	141.6	141.9
1994	141.3	142.1	142.5	144.2	144.7	144.7	144.0	144.7	145.0	145.2	145.3	146.0
1995	146.0	146.9	147.5	149.0	149.6	149.8	149.1	149.9	150.6	149.8	149.8	150.7
1996	150.2	150.9	151.5	152.6	152.9	153.0	152.4	153.1	153.8	153.8	153.9	154.4
1997	154.4	155.0	155.4	156.3	156.9	157.5	157.5	158.5	159.3	159.5	159.6	160.0
1998	159.5	160.3	160.8	162.6	163.5	163.4	163.0	163.7	164.4	164.5	164.4	164.4
1999	163.4	163.7	164.1	165.2	165.6	165.6	165.1	165.5	166.2	166.5	166.7	167.3

Data © HMSO

1 The RPI in June 1993 was:

   a 139.3 ☐   **c** 141.1 ☐

   b 141.0 ☐   **d** 140.7 ☐

2 How much did the RPI increase between January 1990 and January 1992?

3 Fill in the missing number to work out the rate of inflation in January 1998.

$$\frac{\cdots - 154.4}{154.4} \times 100\%$$

4 Look at the figures for each January. In which year was the rate of inflation greatest?

GRADE BOOSTER

Always double-check figures that you have read from tables.

Collecting and organising data

> *Organisations need to make plans. To help them make decisions they need* **data** *(facts and figures).*

If an organisation collects its own data, that is **primary** data.

If they use data gathered by someone else, e.g. information from a census, that is **secondary** data.

Data can be collected in several ways:

- observation, e.g. counting traffic
- experiment, e.g. is revision more effective when there is background music?
- questionnaire, e.g. people's shopping habits
- survey, e.g. use of leisure facilities
- from secondary sources (printed tables, the internet).

Once the data have been collected, you have to process them to make them easy to understand. A list of figures in no particular order is not easy to take in.

Example

The number of hours 20 students spent watching TV last week is as follows:

21 13 40 26 17 5 18 23 16 38 12 2 17 15 21 28 19 0 12 22

Put the data in a grouped frequency table.

number of hours	tally	frequency
0–4	||	2
5–9			1
10–14	|||	3
15–19	‖‖		6
20–24	‖‖	4
25+	‖‖	4

The data have been grouped in **class intervals**, size 5, apart from the last group of 25 or more, which goes up to 38.

You should choose the class intervals so that there are about 5 to 10 groups altogether.

Question Bank 73

Use the following data for questions 1–4.
The heights of some students in Year 10 were measured to the nearest cm as follows.

132	144	151	133	139	156	164	168	147	173
151	138	166	179	182	157	175	169	149	156
167	178	164	172	179	171	158	163	172	170

1 How many students were measured?

2 What was the height of the shortest student?

3 How tall was the tallest student?

4 The data are to be put in a frequency table. Suggest suitable classes so that there are six groups altogether.

5 The lengths of 30 earthworms were measured in centimetres and the results were as follows.

length l (cm)	tally	frequency
$6.0 \leq l < 8.0$	|||	
$8.0 \leq l < 10.0$	ЖН I	
$10.0 \leq l < 12.0$	ЖН |||	
$12.0 \leq l < 14.0$	ЖН ||||	
$14.0 \leq l < 16.0$	|||	
$18.0 \leq l < 20.0$			

a How many worms are in the $14.0 \leq l < 16.0$ group?

b Complete the frequency column.

GRADE BOOSTER

You can use the grouped frequency table chart to draw a diagram. Diagrams are a useful way of presenting data because they're easy to interpret.

Representing data

Tables of figures are not always easy to understand. Diagrams are much easier to appreciate.

Pie charts are particularly useful for representing non-numerical data, such as colours, sporting activities, languages, etc.

Example

In a survey 600 people were asked where they intended to take their next holiday. The results are shown in the table.

destination	number of people
USA and Caribbean	120
Europe	275
Britain	85
Asia	72
Africa	48

The angles for the pie chart are:

USA and Caribbean $\frac{120}{600} \times 360° = 72°$ (There are 360° to divide up according to the size of each group.)

Europe $\frac{275}{600} \times 360° = 165°$ Britain $\frac{85}{600} \times 360° = 51°$ Asia $\frac{72}{600} \times 360° = 43°$

Africa $\frac{48}{600} \times 360° = 29°$ (round to nearest degree)

Pictograms

In these a symbol is used to represent a certain number of items. This pictogram shows what TV services 100 householders use.

Key ☐ = 5 householders

Satellite ☐☐☐☐
Cable ☐☐☐☐☐☐
Terrestrial only ☐☐☐☐☐☐☐☐
None ☐

Frequency diagrams can be used to illustrate data from a frequency table. This diagram illustrates the data, on page 154, on the number of hours 20 students spent watching television.

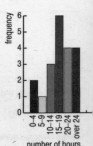

Question Bank 74

1 30 children were asked to choose a breakfast cereal. 15 children chose Sugar Flakes; 10 chose Wheety Bangs and 5 chose Ricicles.

The results are displayed on a pie chart. The angles on the pie chart are:

a 200°, 100°, 60° ☐   **c** 90°, 60°, 30° ☐

b 180°, 100°, 50° ☐   **d** 180°, 120°, 60° ☐

2 The pictogram shows the sales of cars for the month of August at a dealer's.

Model T ☐☐☐☐☐   Key ☐ = 1 car

Model S ☐☐☐

Model E ☐☐☐☐

How many cars did the dealer sell in August?

3 Look at the diagram then answer the question below.

This frequency diagram shows the number of days absent per term for the students in a class at a sixth form college.

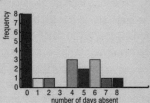

True or false?

a There are 30 students in the class.

b Half the students were absent two days or fewer during the term.

4 Sadie drew this pie chart to show how she uses her monthly salary of £1100.

The angle for the mortgage sector is 120°.
How much is Sadie's mortgage each month?

Scatter graphs

You can use a scatter graph to find out if there is any connection, or **correlation**, between two variables, such as shoe size and height.

Example

Antonio, an ice cream salesman, recorded the midday temperature and his daily sales for a fortnight. The readings are shown in this scatter graph.

(Notice there are about the same number of points above and below the line.)

The graph shows that the higher the temperature, the more ice cream is sold, i.e. there is a strong **positive correlation** between the two variables.

The line of best fit has a *positive* gradient.

You can use the line of best fit to estimate a missing value. For example, one point on the graph is missing. Antonio sold 20 litres of ice cream on that day, but he forgot to record the temperature. What do think the temperature was on that day? (answer: about 23°C)

If there is **no correlation** (zero correlation), the graph looks like this.

You can't draw a line of best fit – there isn't one!

If there is strong **negative correlation**, the graph looks like this.

The line of best fit has a negative gradient.

As the price of chocolate biscuits increases, the number sold decreases.

A graph indicating weak negative correlation looks like this.

Question Bank 75

1 Ten students took Paper 1 and Paper 2 in a
   maths exam. Their results are shown on this
   scatter graph with the line of best fit drawn
   on it.

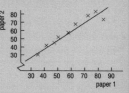

   Floella scored 70% on Paper 1, but she missed Paper 2. What mark do
   you think she might have scored on Paper 2?

2 What sort of correlation does this scatter graph show?

   a strong positive   ☐

   b weak positive   ☐

   c strong negative   ☐

   d weak negative   ☐

3 What sort of correlation (positive, negative or zero) do you think there
   might be between these pairs of variables?

   a Hours of daylight and rate of growth in plants   ☐

   b Number of cars on road and average journey times   ☐

   c Height of a 10-year-old and reading ability   ☐

   d Price of a car and its age   ☐

   e Heights and weights of 10-year-olds   ☐

GRADE BOOSTER

**Get to know what sort of correlation – positive, negative or zero – a
scatter graph shows.**

Mean and median 1

> *Raw (unprocessed) data are not very useful. You need to look at the data and extract information from them. One useful piece of information you can work out is the **average**.*

An average is a typical value that sums up a set of figures, e.g. the average weight of a new-born baby is about 3.3kg.

In fact there are three different sorts of average, each useful in a different way.

- **The mean.** To find the mean, add up all the data and divide by the number of items.

- **The median.** Arrange the data in order and take the middle value. If there are two middle values, the median is half-way between them.

- **The mode.** The mode is the most popular value – that is, the one that occurs most often (see page 164).

Example

A small firm has eight employees. Their annual earnings are:

£12 000 £15 500 £16 000 £16 000 £18 500 £22 000 £25 000 £40 000

$$\text{mean} = \frac{£(12000 + 15500 + 16000 + 16000 + 18500 + 22000 + 25000 + 40000)}{8}$$

$$= £20 625$$

$$\text{median} = \frac{£16000 + £18500}{2} = £17 250$$

When you calculate the mean you use all of the data, but the mean is affected by the large salary at the top end.

The median gives a better idea of the typical salary, as it is the central value.

Question Bank 76

1 The night-time temperatures, in degrees Celsius, on the first ten days of November were as follows:

12°   10°   11°   6°   5°   5°   6°   8°   5°   2°

What was the mean?

2 The times, in hours, eight students spent on their homework were:

$2\frac{1}{2}$ 1   3   2 $1\frac{1}{2}$ 2 $\frac{1}{2}$ 0

What was the median?

3 Ten students did a maths test, which was marked out of 20.

The mean mark was 12.5.

What was the total mark for the ten students?

4 Write down five different numbers whose mean and median are both equal to 4.

5 At Brightpool the mean number of sunny days in June over nine years was 11. The next year was exceptionally hot and dry and the mean number of sunny days increased to 12 for all ten years.

How many sunny days were there in the tenth year?

Mean and median 2

> When there is a large amount of data, it is put into a **grouped frequency table**, e.g. the heights of 50 Year 11 students on page 164.

You can't *calculate* the mean since you don't know the individual heights, but you can *estimate* it.

Estimating the mean

Add two more columns to the table, headed 'Midpoint' and 'Midpoint × frequency'.

Height	Number of students (frequency)
145–150	1
150–155	2
155–160	8
160–165	24
165–170	13
170–175	2

Height	Number of students (frequency)	Midpoint	Midpoint × frequency
145–150	1	147.5	147.5
150–155	2	152.5	305
155–160	8	157.5	1260
160–165	24	162.5	3900
165–170	13	167.5	2177.5
170–175	2	172.5	345
Total	50		8135

There are 8 students in the 155–160 group. Assume that the total height of the 8 students is 8 × the midpoint value, which is $8 \times 157.5 = 1260$.

Do the same for all the groups, then add these totals to get 8135.

Estimated mean $= \dfrac{8135}{50} = 162.7$ cm

You can't pick out the median because you don't know what the 25th value is, but you can estimate it.

Estimating the median

The median is the 25th value. There are 11 $(= 1 + 2 + 8)$ values in the first three groups, so the 25th value will be the $(25 - 11)$th $= 14$th value in the 160–165 group. There are 24 students in this group, and the group is 5 cm wide; so take $\dfrac{14}{24}$ of 5 cm $= 2.9166...$ cm and add it to 160 cm, the lower boundary of the group. Estimated median $= 160 + 2.9166... = 163$ cm to nearest cm.

Question Bank 77

Use this cumulative frequency table to answer the questions.

House prices in Easthampton, week ending 17 March 2001

Price (£ thousands)	Frequency	Cumulative	Midpoint frequency	Midpoint × frequency
0–100	3	3	50	150
100–150	6	9	125	750
150–200	17	26	175	4550
200–250	24	50	225	5400
250–300	19	69	275	5225
300–350	12			3990
350–400	6			2250
400–450	2		425	850
450–500	1	90	475	475
Total	90			23 460

1 What are the missing numbers in the cumulative frequency column?

2 What are the missing numbers in the midpoint column?

3 The correct calculation for estimating the mean is:

a $\dfrac{475\,000}{90}$ ☐   **c** $\dfrac{23\,460}{90}$ ☐

b $275\,000 \times 90$ ☐   **d** $\dfrac{23\,460\,000}{90}$ ☐

4 True or false?

   The median price is in the 250–300 thousand group.

GRADE BOOSTER

Practise estimating the mean and the median from a grouped frequency table.

Range and modal class

As well as knowing the average of a set of data, it's useful to know how spread out it is. The **range** tells you the spread of a set of data.

Range = largest value − smallest value

Example

Two groups of five Year 13 students took a French test.
Their marks were as follows.

Group 1	51	45	39	63	76
Group 2	86	59	61	45	23

The mean mark for both groups is 54.8, but the two groups performed differently.

Range for Group 1 = 76 − 39 = 37   Range for Group 2 = 86 − 23 = 63

Group 1 had more uniform results. The range was much bigger in Group 2, indicating a more uneven performance.

The **mode** is the third sort of average. It is the most frequently occurring value. It is easily picked out if you have the raw data to look at. Sometimes, however, you only have the processed data in the form of a grouped frequency table.

Example

The heights in cm of 50 Year 11 students are given below.

Height	Number of students (frequency)
145–150	1
150–155	2
155–160	8
160–165	24
165–170	13
170–175	2

The group 160–165 cm has the largest number of students, but you don't know the individual heights of the 24 students in that group. You can't say what the mode is, but you can give the **modal group**: 160–165 cm.

Question Bank 78

1 12 children queued up to see Santa. Their ages were as follows:

5 7 6 3 1 2 4 8 3 2 5 4

What was the range of their ages?

2 The frequency diagram shows the length
of time people had waited to be served
at a post office.

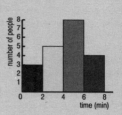

What is the modal group?

3 Five numbers have a range of 20. Four of the numbers are 6, 11, 17 and 25.

What two values could the fifth number have?

4 Make your choice from the answers below.

In ten matches Manchester Rovers scored 15 goals.
The range was 5 and the median was 1.

Which of the following are possible numbers of goals scored?

(i)	0	0	0	0	0	2	2	3	3	5
(ii)	0	0	0	1	1	1	2	2	3	5
(iii)	0	0	1	1	1	1	2	2	3	5
(iv)	0	0	1	1	1	1	2	2	2	5

a (i) and (ii) only ☐

b (iii) only ☐

c (i), (ii) and (iv) only ☐

d (iv) only ☐

GRADE BOOSTER

When you find the range, double-check that you have the correct
largest and smallest values.

Stem-and-leaf diagrams

Stem-and-leaf diagrams are not pictures of stems and leaves – they'd be much prettier if they were! They're a quick way of arranging data in order to show some of the important things about them.

Here are the marks gained by 15 students in a history test:

73   45   62   86   77   50   41   68   88   57   66   49   75   64   53

To put them in a stem-and-leaf diagram, separate each mark into its tens and units digits. The tens digits make the stem.

```
8
7
6
5
4
```

The units digits make the leaves. Here are the leaves from the first five marks.

```
8 | 6
7 | 3   7
6 | 2
5 |
4 | 5
```

Continue adding the leaves until all the marks are entered, then rearrange the leaves in order.

```
8 | 6   8
7 | 3   5   7
6 | 2   4   6   8        Key 4 | 1 means 41
5 | 0   3   7
4 | 1   5   9
```

The modal group is 60–69cm and the median is the middle value, 64.

Two sets of related data can be shown in a back-to-back stem-and-leaf table. Here are the English marks of the same 15 students entered in a back-to-back stem-and-leaf diagram.

```
Key (English)        3   1 | 8 | 6   8
3 | 6 means 63       7   2 | 7 | 3   5   7
                     4   3 | 6 | 2   4   6   8
          7   6   6   5   2 | 5 | 0   3   7        Key (History)
              8   7   2   1 | 4 | 1   5   9        4 | 1 means 41
```

Question Bank 79

Use this stem-and-leaf diagram to answer the questions.

The heights, in cm, of 16-year-old boys and girls are shown in the diagram.

			Boys				Girls								

Key (boys)
217 means 172 cm

Key (girls)
17 | 0 means 170 cm

				2	0	18									
9	8	5	5	5	3	2	17	0	1						
		8	7	4	2	0	16	1	2	3	5	5	6	8	9
					9	15	4	4	5	6	7	8			

1 How many girls were measured?

2 What was the median height for the boys?

3 What was the median height for the girls?

4 True or false?

The range of the boys' heights was greater than the range of the girls' heights.

5 True or false?

The modal group for the girls is 150–159 cm.

GRADE BOOSTER

Don't forget the last step – putting the leaves in order.

Cumulative frequency

Take this topic step by step. **Cumulative** means increasing bit by bit and the **frequency** is just the number of people or things in any particular group.

This frequency table shows the total spent by 80 shoppers at Byrite's Superstore.

Amount (£)	Frequency
0–20	11
over 20–40	13
over 40–60	19
over 60–80	17
over 80–100	10
over 100–120	6
over 120–140	4

How many customers spent £40 or less?

11 customers spent £20 or less and 13 spent £40 or less, so 11 + 13 = 24 customers spent £40 or less.

24 is a **cumulative frequency**, the total of the frequencies up to £40.

To work out the other cumulative frequencies, put a third column in the table.

Amount (£)	Frequency	Cumulative frequency
0–20	11	11
over 20–40	13	24
over 40–60	19	43
over 60–80	17	60
over 80–100	10	70
over 100–120	6	76
over 120–140	4	80

Check that the last cumulative frequency (80) is equal to the total number of shoppers, i.e. the total of the frequency column.

When you plot a graph of the amount spent against the cumulative frequency, you get an S–shaped curve (see p 172).

You can read off an estimate of the median, £58, from the half-way point on the curve.

You can also answer questions such as: 'How many customers spent more than £70?'

Question Bank 80

1 Postman Pete made a note of the number of letters he delivered to each of the 200 houses on his round. The results are shown in the table.

Number of letters	Frequency	Cumulative frequency
0–2	75	75
3–5	80	
6–8	24	179
9–11	16	
12 or more	5	

Complete the cumulative frequency column.

2 This cumulative frequency curve shows the speeds, in m.p.h., of cars passing a radar speed detector.

   a How many cars were there?

   b Estimate the median speed (use the dotted lines on the graph).

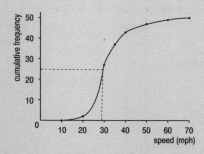

Quartiles and the interquartile range

One very large or very small value has a big effect on the range (see page 164). The interquartile range is another way of measuring the spread that is not affected by extreme values.

To find the interquartile range, divide the data into four quarters.

■ One quarter, or 25%, of the values are less than or equal to the **lower quartile.**

■ Half, or 50%, of the values are less than or equal to the **median**.

■ Three-quarters, or 75% of the values are less than or equal to the **upper quartile.**

The **interquartile range** is the difference between the upper and lower quartiles. It tells you the spread of the middle 50% of the data.

For example, the number of days absent of each of 20 students during the autumn term was as follows.

0 0 0 0 0 | 0 0 0 0 0 | 0 0 1 1 1 | 1 2 2 5 10

  lower quartile   median   upper quartile

    is 0   is 0   is 1

(divide the data into quarters)

Range = 10 − 0 = 10
Interquartile range = 1 − 0 = 1
Mean = 23 ÷ 20 = 1.15
Mode = 0

Which of these statistics gives a realistic idea of the number of absences?

■ The range does not: most students had no absences.

■ The median doesn't help much either, although it does tell you that at least half the students were never away.

■ The interquartile range shows that the middle 50% of the students had either 0 or 1 absences each.

■ The mean tells you that the absence rate was low and the mode shows that the group of students who were never absent is bigger than the group of students who had one or more absences.

Question Bank 81

Use the following data to answer questions 1–7.

16 students were each asked how many brothers and sisters they had.
Their answers were as follows:

  0 0 0 1 1 1 1 1 1 1 1 2 2 2 3 5

For each of questions 1–6, answer true or false.

1 The range is 4.

2 The median is 1.

3 The lower quartile is 0.

4 The upper quartile is 2.

5 The interquartile range is 1.

6 The mode is 1.

7 Why isn't the range a good measure of the spread in this case?

GRADE BOOSTER

You get marks for saying if a statistic represents the data well or not.

Box plots

*You can use a **box plot** (sometimes called a box-and-whisker diagram) to show how the data are spread.*

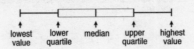

You can find the upper and lower quartiles from a cumulative frequency curve.

Here is the cumulative frequency curve of the amounts spent by shoppers at the Byrite Superstore (see page 168).

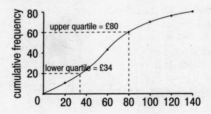

Find the lower quartile by drawing a horizontal line from 20 on the cumulative frequency axis to the curve. From this point draw a vertical line down to the vertical axis and read off the lower quartile = £34.

Find the upper quartile in the same way, starting from 60 on the cumulative frequency axis. The upper quartile = £80.

The interquartile range = £80 − £34 = £46.

The box plot looks like this.

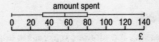

Question Bank 82

1 The box plot shows the times of 100 runners in a marathon.

Estimate:

  a the median time

  b the interquartile range

  c the range

2 120 students took a GCSE maths examination.

The lowest mark was 11% and the highest mark was 96%.

The median was 53% and the upper and lower quartiles were 43% and 61% respectively.

Select the correct box plot below.

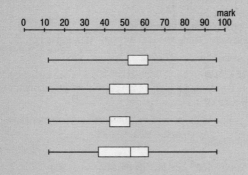

GRADE BOOSTER

Take care to position the upper and lower quartiles and the median correctly on a box plot.

Line graphs and moving averages

*Data are sometimes displayed on a line graph, where points are plotted and joined with straight lines. This is the sort of graph that is used to show changes over time and is often called a **time series**.*

Sales records are often displayed on a time series, as in this example.

Antonio's quarterly ice cream sales (litres)

Spring 1999	1000	Spring 2000	900	Spring 2001	950
Summer	1350	Summer	1450	Summer	1550
Autumn	1150	Autumn	1200	Autumn	1300
Winter	700	Winter	800	Winter	800

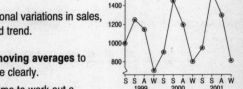

The graph shows seasonal variations in sales, but also a slight upward trend.

■ You can work out **moving averages** to show the trend more clearly.

Use four values each time to work out a four-point moving average.

First four-point average $= \dfrac{1000 + 1350 + 1150 + 700}{4} = 1050$

Second four-point average $= \dfrac{1350 + 1150 + 700 + 900}{4} = 1025$

(discard the first value, 1000, and include the fifth value, 900)

Third four-point average $= \dfrac{1150 + 700 + 900 + 1450}{4} = 1050$

(discard 1350 and include 1450)
and so on.

There are six more to work out. Try to do them yourself. You should get:
1062.5, 1087.5, 1100, 1125, 1150, 1150.

Plot them on the time series as circled dots.

Question Bank 83

1. Harry Sparks' electricity bill seemed to be going through the roof. He decided to work out the four-point moving averages to see the trend.

   His last six quarterly bills are given in the table.

Sep 2000	Dec 2000	Mar 2001	Jun 2001	Sep 2001	Dec 2001
£150	£250	£350	£250	£250	£350

   Is each of the following statements true or false?

   a The first four-point moving average is £250

   b The second four-point moving average is £270

   c The last four-point moving average is £300

Read the following, then answer questions 2–4.

   Doug is a double-glazing salesman. He likes to work out his quarterly moving averages, as he's sure he's getting better at selling.

	2000				2001		
Spring	Summer	Autumn	Winter	Spring	Summer	Autumn	Winter
39	35	36	50	42	36	37	52

2. How many four-point moving averages can Doug work out from the table?

3. True or false?

   The first four-point average is 40.

4. Fill in the missing figures in this calculation for the Summer 2001 moving average.

$$\frac{a + 50 + 42 + b}{c}$$

GRADE BOOSTER

Don't be scared of moving averages. You can pin them down. Practise working some out until you get the hang of them.

Two-way tables

Two-way tables are used to show two sets of data about the same group of people or things. Let's look at some examples to show you how they work.

a Kate wrote down the eye colour and natural hair colour of everyone in her class.

Hair

		Blond	Brown	Red	Black	Total
Eyes	Blue	4	3	1	2	10
	Brown	1	4	0	5	10
	Hazel	4	6	1	0	11
	Total	9	13	2	7	31

From the table you can see that, for example, 5 students have brown eyes and black hair, and that there are 31 students in the class.

b Reed's Bookshop keeps a record of its weekly sales. During the week starting 12 November they sold 83 hardback books, 68 of which were non-fiction, and 196 paperback fiction books. They sold 312 books altogether that week.

How many non-fiction paperbacks were sold?

Put the data in a two-way table.

	Fiction	Non-fiction	Total
Hardback		68	83
Paperback	196		
Total			312

You can work out the missing entries in the table.
Total number of paperbacks = 312 − 83 = 229
Total number of non-fiction paperbacks = 229 − 196 = 33
Work out the other entries in the same way.
The completed table looks like this:

	Fiction	Non-fiction	Total
Hardback	15	68	83
Paperback	196	33	229
Total	211	101	312

Question Bank 84

The members of Whitehaven Youth Club were asked to choose a Christmas activity. Some of the data are entered in the table below.

	Ice skating	Bowling	Cinema	Total
Boys	3	9		19
Girls	5		7	18
Total				

Use the table to answer these questions.

1 How many members are in the club?

2 How many boys chose the cinema?

3 How many people altogether wanted to go bowling?

4 Which activity was least popular among the boys?

5 Which activity was most preferred by the girls?

Comparing and interpreting data

> *It's no use collecting and organising data and then putting them on a shelf to gather dust. You've got to use them!*

This table gives the times a group of 15 boys and 13 girls took to run 100 metres.

				Time (s)				
Boys	10.9	11.6	12.2	10.8	12.5	10.6	11.9	11.3
	11.5	12.6	11.7	10.7	11.1	11.7	12.8	
Girls	11.3	11.6	12.8	12.4	13.1	11.9	12.2	13.3
	11.8	12.7	12.2	13.0	11.7			

Compare the performances of the boys and girls.

To do this you could find the mean time, the range and the median for each group.

You could put the times in a stem-and-leaf table and then you could say what you noticed.

Boys' mean time = 11.6s to nearest tenth

Girls' mean time = 12.3s to nearest tenth

Range of boy's times = 2.2s

Range of girls' times = 2.0s

				Boys					**Girls**				
Key (boys)				9	8	7	6	10					
6 | 10 means 10.6	9	7	7	6	5	3	1	11	3	6	7	8	9
				8	6	5	2	12	2	2	4	7	8
Key (girls) 11 | 3 means 11.3								13	0	1	3		

From the stem-and-leaf diagram, you can read off the medians.

Boys' median time = 11.6s

Girls' median time = 12.2s

You might make these observations:

■ The boys were faster than the girls by about 1 second on average.

■ The range of the girls' times was slightly less than for the boys, so their performances were slightly more consistent.

Question Bank 85

The mean monthly temperatures, in °C, in London and Moscow
are as follows:

	J	F	M	A	M	J	J	A	S	O	N	D
London	4	5	7	9	12	16	18	17	15	11	8	5
Moscow	−13	−10	−4	6	13	16	18	17	12	6	−1	−7

1 Match each city with its mean and median temperatures.

   a Mean = 11°C

   b Mean = 4°C

   c Median = 6°C

   d Median = 10°C

2 What is the temperature range in Moscow?

3 What is the temperature range in London?

4 True or false?

   a London has a less temperate climate than Moscow

   b The temperature range in Moscow is more than twice that in London

   c Winters are much colder in Moscow

   d Summers are much hotter in London

GRADE BOOSTER

If you're asked to compare two sets of data, start by finding some
statistics such as the averages and the range; or the interquartile
range if the data have one or more unusually large or small values.
Make some conclusions and back them up with the statistics.

The probability scale

The probability of this topic coming up in the exam is 1!

■ The probability of something happening tells you how likely it is to occur.

How likely are these events?

a Someone you know will win the jackpot in the National Lottery.

b You will have a lie-in on Sunday.

c You will take GCSE maths this summer.

A is unlikely, B is quite likely and C is very likely.

■ Probability is measured on a scale from 0 to 1.

Here are events A, B and C on the scale:

A	B	C
0	0.5	1
Unlikely	Quite likely	Very likely

An event with a probability of 0 is impossible – e.g. scoring 13 with two dice.

An event with a probability of 1 is certain, e.g. if this month is June, next month will be July.

■ Some probabilities can be calculated.

Example

A card is drawn from a pack of 52 playing cards. What is the probability that it is:

a a red card   **b** a diamond   **c** the 7 of clubs?

a Half the cards are red, so P(red card) $= \frac{26}{52} = \frac{1}{2}$

b There are 13 diamonds, so P(diamond) $= \frac{13}{52} = \frac{1}{4}$

c There is only one 7 of clubs, so P(7 of clubs) $= \frac{1}{52}$

Question Bank 86

1 What is the probability that you will live to the year 3000?

2 If you throw a coin 10 times, will you get 5 heads?

3 In her purse, Rana has three 10p coins, two 20p coins and one 50p coin.
   If she takes out a coin without looking, the probability that it is a 20p coin is:

   a $\frac{2}{3}$ ☐   c $\frac{1}{3}$ ☐

   b $\frac{1}{2}$ ☐   d $\frac{1}{4}$ ☐

4 There are 37 numbers on a roulette wheel (0, 1, 2, ... 36).
   If Pascal bets on the 7, what is the probability he wins?

5 Match the events a–e with their probabilities (i)–(v) as listed below:

   a Throwing a six with a fair dice ☐

   b Throwing an even number with a fair dice ☐

   c Drawing an ace from a pack of 52 cards ☐

   d The name of a day of the week starting with 'S' ☐

   e Without looking, taking a soft-centred chocolate from a box
     containing 7 soft centres and 13 hard centres. ☐

(i) $\frac{1}{2}$ (ii) $\frac{7}{20}$ (iii) $\frac{1}{13}$ (iv) $\frac{1}{6}$ (v) $\frac{2}{7}$

GRADE BOOSTER

Remember:

$$\text{probability} = \frac{\text{number of ways outcome you want can happen}}{\text{total number of possible outcomes}}$$

Estimating probabilities

You can't always calculate a probability, as some things in life aren't cut and dried.

■ If you can't calculate a probability, you can often *estimate* it.

Examples

1 The People's Party (PP) want to know if they will win the general election.

1000 voters are asked to state their voting intention and 653 say they will vote for the PP.

a What is the probability of a voter choosing the PP?

b How many votes can the PP expect from an electorate of 40 million voters?

a $\frac{653}{1000}$ = 65.3%, so P(voter choosing the PP) is 0.653.

b 65.3% × 40 000 000 = 26 120 000

$\quad\quad\quad\quad\quad\quad\quad\quad\quad = 26$ million to 2 s.f.

2 Sayed drops a drawing pin 100 times. It lands 'point-up' 73 times. What is the probability of the pin landing point-up the next time?

The **relative frequency** of landing point up is $\frac{73}{100}$.

You can use the relative frequency as an estimate of the probability of the pin landing point–up.

P(point up) = $\frac{73}{100}$ = 0.73

■ Probabilities can be estimated from past data.

Suppose you want to know if people are more likely to die in winter than in summer.

You could examine the register of deaths in your district over the last 20 years and make an estimate of the probability of a person dying in winter.

Question Bank 87

1 A fair dice is rolled 90 times. How many times would you expect to get a six?

2 The spinner shown here is spun 200 times.

How many times would you expect to get an odd number?

a 60 ☐   c 3 ☐

b 120 ☐   d 66 ☐

3 Janie counts the number of matches in ten boxes. She finds these numbers:

   32   30   31   33   29   30   31   32   30   32

   One box is selected at random. What is the probability that it contains more than 30 matches?

4 25% of the marbles in a bag are green. Sam takes out 20 marbles. How many of them are likely to be green?

5 Ben is late one day out of five. The autumn term has 70 days. How many times is Ben likely to be late during the term?

GRADE BOOSTER

If the experiment is repeated lots of times, the estimated probability will be more reliable.

Listing outcomes

If you list all the outcomes of an event, it can help you work out the probabilities.

■ Single events

Percy has two coins of each denomination in his pocket. He takes out one coin. What is the probability that it is worth at least 50p?

List the coins:

1p, 1p, 2p, 2p, 5p, 5p, 10p, 10p, 20p, 20p, 50p, 50p, £1, £1, £2, £2

There are 16 coins and 6 of them are worth 50p or more.

So, $P(\text{50p or more}) = \frac{6}{16} = \frac{3}{8}$

■ Two successive events

Suppose you throw a coin and roll a dice.

List all the possible outcomes:

6H	5H	4H	3H	2H	1H
6T	5T	4T	3T	2T	1T

All these outcomes are equally likely, so the probability of each one is $\frac{1}{12}$.

If you throw two dice, there are a lot of possible outcomes.
They are best shown in a table.

```
                6  ×  ×  ×  ×  ×  ×
Score on        5  ×  ×  ×  ×  ×  ×        There are 36
second dice     4  ×  ×  ×  ×  ×  ×        different possible outcomes.
                3  ×  ×  ×  ×  ×  ×  ←─ This point represents
                2  ×  ×  ×  ×  ×  ×        a score of 6 on the first
                1  ×  ×  ×  ×  ×  ×        and 3 on the second dice.
                   1  2  3  4  5  6
                   Score on first dice
```

The probability of each of the 36 outcomes is $\frac{1}{36}$.

The total of the probabilities of all the 36 outcomes is $36 \times \frac{1}{36} = 1$.

Question Bank 88

1 How many ways can you score 11 with two dice?

2 True or false?

   The probability of scoring 11 with two dice is $\frac{1}{18}$.

3 How many ways are there of scoring 7 with two dice?

   a 2 ☐

   b 4 ☐

   c 6 ☐

   d 8 ☐

4 True or false?

   The probability of scoring 12 with two dice is lower than the probability of getting any other score.

5 Complete this list of possible outcomes when three coins are thrown.

   HHH   HHT   **a**___   THH   HTT   THT   **b**___   TTT

6 What is the probability of getting three heads from three coins?

GRADE BOOSTER

It's always a good idea to list the outcomes. It helps you see what the possibilities are.

185

Exclusive events

In probability theory, 'exclusive' has a technical meaning – an exclusive event isn't a garden party at Buckingham Palace!

■ If you toss a coin once, you cannot get a head and a tail. The two events are **mutually exclusive**. They cannot happen at the same time.

$$P(\text{head}) = \frac{1}{2} \text{ and } P(\text{tail}) = \frac{1}{2} \qquad P(\text{head or tail}) = \frac{1}{2} + \frac{1}{2} = 1$$

$$P(\text{head}) = 1 - P(\text{tail}) = 1 - \frac{1}{2} = \frac{1}{2}$$

■ When you roll a dice, the probability of each of the scores 1, 2, 3, 4, 5 and 6 is $\frac{1}{6}$.

$$P(\text{scoring 1, 2, 3, 4, 5 or 6}) = 6 \times \frac{1}{6} = 1$$

$$P(\text{not scoring 6}) = P(\text{scoring 1, 2, 3, 4 or 5}) = 5 \times \frac{1}{6} = \frac{5}{6}$$

$$P(\text{scoring 6}) = 1 - \frac{5}{6} = \frac{1}{6}$$

For mutually exclusive events:

■ the total sum of the probabilities is 1

■ the probability of an event happening is 1 minus the probability of it not happening.

Examples

1 What is the probability of drawing an ace from a pack of cards?

$$P(\text{ace}) = \frac{4}{52} = \frac{1}{13}$$

What is the probability of **not** drawing an ace? $\qquad P(\text{not ace}) = 1 - \frac{1}{13} = \frac{12}{13}$

2 The probability of a wet day in November is $\frac{17}{30}$

$$P(\text{dry day}) = 1 - P(\text{wet day}) = 1 \frac{17}{30} = \frac{13}{30}$$

Question Bank 89

1 A bag contains 4 red sweets, 5 green sweets, 3 yellow sweets and 3 purple sweets. Chloe likes red sweets. What is the probability that she does **not** take a red sweet first time?

a $\frac{4}{15}$ ☐   c $\frac{11}{4}$ ☐

b $\frac{4}{11}$ ☐   d $\frac{11}{15}$ ☐

2 A roulette wheel has the numbers 0–36 (37 numbers in all).

a What is the probability of the ball coming to rest on the 18?

b What is the probability of the ball not coming to rest on the 18?

3 Tom takes a card from a pack of 52 cards. What is the probability that he doesn't get a diamond?

4 The letters of the word 'sunshine' are put in a hat. Jo draws one out.

What is the probability that it is not an 'n'?

5 Ed has these coins in his pocket:

Coin	2p	5p	10p	20p	50p	£1	£2
Number	2	1	2	3	1	5	1

What is the probability that if he takes out a coin at random it will be worth:

a more than £1   b worth less than £1?

GRADE BOOSTER

You can often save time finding a probability by subtracting a probability you know from 1.

Independent events

> When you toss a coin and roll a dice, what you get on the coin has no effect on what you get on the dice. The two events, tossing a coin and rolling a dice, are **independent.**

The 12 possible outcomes of tossing a coin and rolling a dice are listed on page 184. They are all equally likely so the probability of each outcome is $\frac{1}{12}$.

So $P(H,3) = \frac{1}{12}$

The probability of getting a head on the coin $= P(H) = \frac{1}{2}$

The probability of getting a 3 on the dice $= P(3) = \frac{1}{6}$

$$P(H) \times P(3) = \frac{1}{2} \times \frac{1}{6} = \frac{1}{12} \qquad \text{So, } P(H,3) = P(H) \times P(3)$$

■ If two events, A and B, are independent, the probability of them both happening is $P(A) \times P(B)$.

Example

Des rolls two dice. What is the probability that he scores:

a 2 on the first and 1 on the second

b 1 on the first and 2 on the second

c a total of 3 ?

a The events are independent. $P(2) \times P(1) = \frac{1}{6} \times \frac{1}{6} = \frac{1}{36}$

b $P(1) \times P(2) = \frac{1}{6} \times \frac{1}{6} = \frac{1}{36}$

c Des can get a total of 3 from (2, 1) or (1, 2),
so $P(\text{total of 3}) = \frac{1}{36} + \frac{1}{36} = \frac{2}{36} = \frac{1}{18}$

■ If the same result can occur in two different events, **add** the probabilities of the two events to get the probability of the result.

Question Bank 90

Questions 1–4 are all about this spinner.
It has 1 blue, 1 yellow, 1 green and 3 red sections.

1 Dave spins it twice. The probability that he gets 'red' both times is:

  a $\frac{1}{4}$ ☐   **c** $\frac{1}{3}$ ☐

  b 1. ☐   **d** $\frac{1}{12}$ ☐

2 Emma spins it twice. The probability that she gets 'yellow' both times is:

  a $\frac{1}{12}$ ☐   **c** $\frac{1}{36}$ ☐

  b 1 ☐   **d** $\frac{1}{9}$ ☐

3 Fergus spins it twice. The probability that he gets 'red' first and then 'blue' is:

  a $\frac{1}{2}$ ☐   **c** $\frac{1}{4}$ ☐

  b 1 ☐   **d** $\frac{1}{12}$ ☐

4 Gracie spins it twice. The probability that she gets 'red' and 'green' *in any order* is:

  a $\frac{1}{6}$ ☐   **c** $\frac{1}{36}$ ☐

  b 1 ☐   **d** $\frac{1}{12}$ ☐

GRADE BOOSTER

When you multiply two probabilities, the answer is *smaller* than the separate probabilities. When you add, the answer is *bigger*. You can use this to help you if you're not sure whether to add or multiply.

189

Tree diagrams 1

Tree diagrams are a neat way of showing the outcomes of two or more events.

The probability of a sunny day in June is $\frac{1}{3}$. What is the probability that:

a both days of a weekend will be sunny **b** at least one day will be sunny?

Draw the tree.

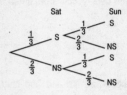

Write the outcomes at the end of the branches.
Write the probabilities on the branches.
(The probability of a day not being sunny is $1 - P(S) = \frac{2}{3}$)

List the outcomes and their probabilities.

	Outcome	Probability
	S, S	$\frac{1}{3} \times \frac{1}{3} = \frac{1}{9}$
	S, not S	$\frac{1}{3} \times \frac{2}{3} = \frac{2}{9}$
	not S, S	$\frac{2}{3} \times \frac{1}{3} = \frac{2}{9}$
	not S, not S	$\frac{2}{3} \times \frac{2}{3} = \frac{4}{9}$

Total $= \frac{9}{9} = 1$

(Check that the total of all the probabilities is 1.)

Note: **Multiply** the probabilities along the branches.
Add the probabilities for the different ways of getting the result.

a $P(S, S) = \frac{1}{9}$

b $P(\text{one sunny day}) = \frac{2}{9} + \frac{2}{9} = \frac{4}{9}$

Question Bank 91

The probability that a runner bean germinates is 0.9. Issie plants two beans.

The tree diagram shows the outcomes. (G means 'germinates'; NG means 'doesn't germinate'.)

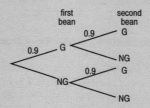

1 List all the different outcomes as (G, G), etc.

2 Fill in the missing probabilities on the diagram.

3 The probability that both beans germinate is:

   a 0.9 ☐   **b** 0.81 ☐   **c** 1.8 ☐   **d** 8.1 ☐

4 The probability that neither bean germinates is:

   a 0.1 ☐   **b** 0.9 ☐   **c** 0.01 ☐   **d** 0.2 ☐

5 The probability that just one bean germinates is:

   a 1 ☐   **b** 1.8 ☐   **c** 0.2 ☐   **d** 0.18 ☐

GRADE BOOSTER

If you keep a wide angle between the first two branches, it's easier to draw the rest of the tree.

Tree diagrams 2

Tree diagrams are particularly useful in situations where items are taken out and not replaced.

Harry has a bag of 15 marbles. 8 are blue and 7 are green. He takes out a marble and does not put it back. Then he takes another marble. What is the probability that he gets:

a 2 blue marbles **b** 2 green marbles **c** one of each colour?

For the first marble, $P(B) = \frac{8}{15}$ and $P(G) = \frac{7}{15}$.

For the second marble, the probabilities change. Now, there are only 14 marbles in the bag. If the first one was blue there will be 7 blue and 7 red marbles in the bag. Then $P(B) = \frac{7}{14}$ and $P(G) = \frac{7}{14}$.

If the first marble was green there will be 8 blue and 6 green marbles left in the bag. Then $P(B) = \frac{8}{14}$ and $P(G) = \frac{6}{14}$.

Outcome Probability

B, B	$\frac{8}{15} \times \frac{7}{14} = \frac{56}{210}$
B, G	$\frac{8}{15} \times \frac{7}{14} = \frac{56}{210}$
G, B	$\frac{7}{15} \times \frac{8}{14} = \frac{56}{210}$
G, G	$\frac{7}{15} \times \frac{6}{14} = \frac{42}{210}$ Total $= \frac{210}{210} = 1$

first marble: $\frac{8}{15}$ B, $\frac{7}{15}$ G
second marble: $\frac{7}{14}$ B, $\frac{7}{14}$ G, $\frac{8}{14}$ B, $\frac{6}{14}$ G

Notice that the probabilities on any pair of branches add up to 1.

a $P(B, B) = \frac{56}{210} = \frac{4}{15}$ **b** $P(G, G) = \frac{42}{210} = \frac{1}{5}$

c P(one of each colour) $= \frac{56}{210} + \frac{56}{210} = \frac{112}{210} = \frac{8}{15}$

Question Bank 92

Read the following, then answer questions 1–5.

Jimmy's father sometimes takes him to school in the car. The probability that this happens on any day is $\frac{2}{5}$. If Jimmy doesn't get a lift, he goes on his bike.

If Jimmy cycles on one day, the probability that his father will take him in the car the next day increases to $\frac{4}{5}$. The tree diagram shows the outcomes for Monday and Tuesday. (C means 'car' and B means 'bike'.)

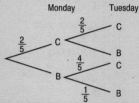

1 What is the probability that Jimmy cycles to school on Monday?

2 Fill in the missing probabilities on the diagram.

3 List all the outcomes as (C, B), etc.

4 The probability that Jimmy gets a lift on both Monday and Tuesday is:

a $\frac{4}{5}$ ☐   b $\frac{4}{25}$ ☐   c $\frac{8}{25}$ ☐   d 0 ☐

5 The probability that Jimmy goes on his bike both days is:

a $\frac{3}{25}$ ☐   b $\frac{18}{25}$ ☐   c $\frac{21}{25}$ ☐   d 1 ☐

GRADE BOOSTER

Remember that probabilities change if an item is not replaced.

Question Bank Answers

Question bank 1
1 8
2 c
3 False
4 −10
5 b
6 −7, −3, 0, 2, 5, 11

Question bank 2
1 1, 2, 3, 4, 6, 9, 12, 18, 36
2 factor
3 9, 18, 27, 36, 45
4 12
5 4 (83, 87, 89, 97)
6 d
7 $2 \times 2 \times 2 \times 2 \times 3$

Question bank 3
1 d
2 0.84
3 58.65
4 0.875
5 $\frac{3}{5}$
6 $\frac{11}{20}$

Question bank 4
1 a (iii)
   b (i)
   c (ii)
2 b, c, d
3 $0.41\dot{6}$
4 b
5 $\frac{2}{9}$, $\frac{1}{4}$, 0.27

Question bank 5
1 $\frac{9}{16}$
2 $\frac{1}{3}$, $\frac{3}{9}$, $\frac{4}{12}$
3 a 20
   b 24
   c 36
4 a

5 $\frac{13}{60}$, $\frac{14}{60}$
6 $\frac{4}{9}$, $\frac{7}{15}$, $\frac{1}{2}$

Question bank 6
1 d
2 $4\frac{1}{5}$
3 $6\frac{7}{8}$
4 a
5 $4\frac{5}{12}$

Question bank 7
1 b
2 $\frac{3}{8}$ of £60
3 $\frac{4}{15}$
4 True
5 8
6 $2\frac{1}{6}$

Question bank 8
1 a 340
   b 0.0052
2 a 1 235 000
   b 500 000
3 d
4 12 000, £13, £8, £150 000
5 a 16.6cm^2
   b 18.0cm

Question bank 9
1 £6000
2 c
3 20
4 6
5 a (ii)
   b (iii)
   c (i)

Question bank 10:
1 c
2 1000.5, 999.5
3 40.5, 39.5

4 b

5 25.3 m/s

Question bank 11
1 −14

2 True

3 19

4 d

5 **a** (iv)
  b (ii)
  c (iii)
  d (i)

Question bank 12
1 a

2 **a** 37.5%
  b 55%

3 **a** (iv)
  b (i)
  c (iii)
  d (ii)

4 d

5 £8030

Question bank 13
1 False

2 c

3 £75

4 1540

5 6.1 cm

Question bank 14
1 **a** (iii)
  b (iv)
  c (i)
  d (ii)

2 b

3 **a** $\frac{11}{20}$
  b 0.55
  c 55%

4 £15, £35

5 False

Question bank 15
1 a

2 9 kg

3 10, 30, 50

4 25% = $\frac{1}{4}$ $33\frac{1}{3}\% = 1:3$
   80% = $\frac{4}{5}$ 120% = 1.2

Question bank 16
1 $7\frac{1}{2}$ min

2 £9

3 a

4 27

5 £43.33

Question bank 17
1 d

2 d

3 9

4 $35 + 21\sqrt{2}$

5 5, 9, ±3

Question bank 18
1 7^{12}

2 3^6

3 a

4 add, subtract

5 $4^5 \times 3^2 \times 2^4$

6 **a** (ii)
  b (iv)
  c (iii)
  d (i)

Question bank 19
1 3×10^8

2 c

3 a

4 2.6×10^9

5 **a** (iii)
  b (ii)
  c (i)
  d (iv)

Question bank 20

1 43100000
2 a
3 2.4×10^9
4 $4.1 \times 10^9 \, cm^2$
5 13

Question bank 21

1 **a** (iv)
   b (i)
   c (ii)
   d (iii)
2 b
3 £2289.80
4 d
5 c

Question bank 22

1 c
2 37 m/s
3 4 km
4 b
5 9.9 g

Question bank 23

1 **a** (iv)
   b (iii)
   c (ii)
   d (i)
2 0
3 **a** True
   b False
4 25
5 $3\frac{1}{3}$

Question bank 24

1 a
2 $3x(x + 2)$
3 **a** (ii)
   b (iv)
   c (i)
   d (iii)
4 $3(c - d)/b$
5 d
6 $v = 430$

Question bank 25

1 $3x + 3 = 50$
2 $4x + 20 = 180$
3 c
4 a

Question bank 26

1 c
2 b
3 9×10^{15}
4 $W = 200 + 80n$
5 $h = 2A/b$

Question bank 27

1 25, 12.5
2 81, 27, 9, 3
3 d
4 25
5 $2n - 1$

Question bank 28

1 b
2 −4
3 $6x^2 + 3xy$
4 a
5 $4x^4$

Question bank 29

1 $5a(2b + 3d)$
2 True
3 b
4 $(2x + y)(3a + b)$
5 d

Question bank 30

1 d
2 16
3 **a** (iv)
   b (iii)
   c (i)
   d (ii)
4 (ii) (should be $10 - 2x + 3 = 21$)
5 −5

Question bank 31

1　a　-2
　　b　0
　　c　1
2　a
3　b
4　a　(i)
　　b　(iv)
　　c　(ii)
　　d　(iii)
5　x-axis at (2,0); y-axis at (0, 4)

Question bank 32

1　(3, 0) and (0, 3)
2　a　(iii)
　　b　(i)
　　c　(iv)
　　d　(ii)
3　a and d
4　c
5　½

Question bank 33

1　$x = 2, y = -1$
2　(1, 4)
3　d
4　b
5　$x = 4, y = 3$

Question bank 34

1　b
2　$a = 2, b = -3$
3　a　(ii)
　　b　(i)
　　c　(iii)
4　d

Question bank 35

1　a　(iii)
　　b　(ii)
　　c　(i)
　　d　(iv)
2　c
3　$6a(2a + b)(2a - b)$
4　$(p - 1)/(p + 4)$
5　$(55 + 44)(55 - 44) = 99 \times 11 = 1089$

Question bank 36

1　a　$x \geq 1$
　　b　$x < -1$
2　d
3　$n > 4$
4　a
5　$-2, -1, 0, 1, 2, 3, 4$

Question bank 37

1　$x + y < 5$
2　c
3　b
4　d

Question bank 38

1　3 and 4
2　d
3　18.5
4　7.7
5　2 and 3

Question bank 39

1　a　77°F
　　b　10°C
2　a　200
　　b　10.30 p.m.
3　210p, 80p
4　a　(ii)
　　b　(iii)
　　c　(i)

Question bank 40

1 9.30
2 15 miles
3 30mph
4 1 hour
5 10min

Question bank 41

1 10s
2 −1m/s^2
3 5m/s
4 10s
5 200m

Question bank 42

1 $(x + 3)(x + 1)$
2 b
3 c
4 0, 1
5 −2, −5

Question bank 43

1 $x^2 + 11x + 12 = 0$
2 False ($\pm\sqrt{5}$)
3 $3(c + 6)(c − 1)$
4 b

Question bank 44

1 3, −1, −3, −3, −1, 3
2 −1.2, 3.2
3 1
4 $(x + 3)(x + 1) = 0$
5 (−3, 0) and (−1, 0)

Question bank 45

1 a (iii)
   b (i)
   c (iv)
   d (ii)
2 −2, −3, −6, −12, 6, 4, 3, 1
3 Reflect in y-axis

Question bank 46

1 b
2 b
3 a (ii)
   b (iii)
   c (i)

Question bank 47

1 $x = 10$; $y = 5$, 12.5
2 d
3 a
4 c
5 £4.08

Question bank 48

1 b, e
2 c
3 93°
4 c
5 perpendicular, CD

Question bank 49

1 50°
2 c
3 b
4 38°, 82°

Question bank 50

1 equilateral
2 c
3 a (iii)
   b (i)
   c (iv)
   d (ii)
4 25°

Question bank 51

1 a trapezium
   b kite
   c rhombus
2 b
3 40°
4 (2, 0)

Question bank 52
1 12
2 45°
3 b
4 135°

Question bank 53
1 20cm
2 17cm
3 b
4 17cm

Question bank 54
1 a
2 b
3 7cm
4 17m

Question bank 55
1 a yes
  b no
  c no
  d yes
2 No (angle not between equal sides)
3 AAS
4 ANB, ANC; BXN, CXN (RHS)
  BLC, CMB; AXB, AXC; AXL, AXH
  (SAS)   LBX, MXC (AAS)

Question bank 56
1 $y = x$
2 $\begin{pmatrix} -4 \\ -3 \end{pmatrix}$
3 (0, 0)
4 90°
5 anticlockwise

Question bank 57
1 b
2 (1, 0)
3 c
4 3

Question bank 58
1 d
2 7.5
3 yes
4 a
5 no

Question bank 59
1 b
2 $^{12}/_{13}$
3 ½
4 4.0
5 11m

Question bank 60
1 b
2 060°
3 a (iii)
  b (i)
  c (ii)
  d (iv)
4 a

Question bank 61
1 65°
2 a (iv)
  b (iii)
  c (ii)
  d (i)
3 c
4 False

Question bank 62
1 75°
2 $x = 35°$, $y = 55°$
3 130°
4 50°

Question bank 63
1 Cone
2 a (ii)
  b (iii)
  c (i)
3 Triangular prism
4 Ball on top of an open cube

Question bank 64

1 d
2 c
3 b
4 1300cm^2

Question bank 65

1 140cm^3
2 b
3 a (iv)
  b (iii)
  c (ii)
  d (i)
4 7.5cm^3

Question bank 66

1 d
2 3
3 a (i)
  b (iv)
4 length
5 a 0
  b 1
  c 3
  d 0

Question bank 67

1 3
2 5
3 c
4 d, e, b, c, a

Question bank 68

1 10
2 True
3 a (iii)
  b (ii)
  c (i)
  d (iv)
4 (2, 2)

Question bank 69

1 b
2 (ii)
3 f

Question bank 70

1 3.5
2 36
3 c
4 d
5 105p per kilo

Question bank 71

1 a Yes
  b No: leading question
  c No
  d No; needs a box for 'other destinations'
2 a, b and d

Question bank 72

1 b
2 16.1
3 159.5
4 1990–1991

Question bank 73

1 30
2 132cm
3 182cm
4 130–139, 140–149, 150–159, 160–169, 170–179, 180–189
5 a 3
  b 3, 6, 8, 9, 3, 1

Question bank 74

1 d
2 12
3 a False
  b True
4 £366.67

Question bank 75

1 75%
2 b
3 **a** positive
  b negative
  c zero
  d negative
  e positive

Question bank 76

1 7°C
2 1¾h
3 125
4 e.g. 1, 3, 4, 5, 7
5 21

Question bank 77

1 81, 87, 89
2 325, 375
3 d
4 False

Question bank 78

1 7 years
2 4–6min
3 5 or 26
4 c

Question bank 79

1 16
2 173cm
3 162.5cm
4 True
5 False

Question bank 80

1 155, 195, 200
2 **a** 50
  b 29mph

Question bank 81

1 False (5)
2 True
3 False (1)
4 True
5 True
6 True
7 distorted by one high value

Question bank 82

1 **a** 260
  b 110
  c 235
2 b

Question bank 83

1 **a** True
  b False (£275)
  c True
2 5
3 True
4 **a** 36
  b 36
  c 4

Question bank 84

1 37
2 7
3 15
4 Ice skating
5 Cinema

Question bank 85

1 London a) and d); Moscow d)and c)
2 31°
3 13°
4 **a** False
  b True
  c True
  d False

Question bank 86
1 0
2 Not necessarily
3 c
4 $\frac{1}{37}$
5 a (iv)
  b (i)
  c (iii)
  d (v)
  e (ii)

Question bank 87
1 15
2 b
3 $\frac{3}{5}$
4 5
5 14

Question bank 88
1 2
2 True
3 c
4 False
5 a HTH
  b TTH
6 $\frac{1}{8}$

Question bank 89
1 d
2 a $\frac{1}{37}$
  b $\frac{36}{37}$
3 $\frac{3}{4}$
4 $\frac{3}{4}$
5 a $\frac{1}{15}$
  b $\frac{14}{15}$

Question bank 90
1 a
2 c
3 d
4 a

Question bank 91
1 (G, G) (G, NG) (NG, G) (NG, NG)
2 0.1 (3 times)
3 b
4 c
5 d

Question bank 92
1 $\frac{3}{5}$
2 $\frac{3}{5}$, $\frac{3}{5}$
3 CC, CB, BC, BB
4 b
5 a

Scoring Grid

Glossary

base   in the number 2^3 the base is 2

bearing   clockwise angle between the North line and a given direction

circumference   distance round a circle

congruent   exactly the same shape and size

correlation   change in one variable corresponding to a change in another variable

cube root   the number which, when multiplied by itself twice, is equal to the given number

cubic   expression or equation with an x^3 term

cumulative frequency   the sum of the frequencies up a certain value of the variable

denominator   the bottom number in a fraction

elevation   view of an object form the front or side

enlargement   making an object larger or smaller

equivalent fraction   a fraction equal to a given fraction with a different numerator and denominator

exclusive events   two events that cannot happen at the same time

expand   multiply out the brackets

exterior angle   angle outside a polygon formed by extending one of the sides

factor   integer that divides exactly into a given integer

factorise   rewrite with brackets

frequency   the number of times an event occurs

gradient   the slope of a line: rise ÷ run

highest common factor   highest number that is a factor of two or more numbers, e.g. HCF of 28 and 42 is 14

identity   an equation that is true for all values of the variables, e.g. $3x(x + y) \equiv 3x^2 + 3xy$

index   in the number 2^3 the index is 3

integer   whole number

intercept   distance between the origin and the point where a graph crosses the y-axis

interior angle   angle inside a polygon

interquartile range   the difference between the upper and lower quartiles

linear equation   one whose graph is a straight line

locus   a line or region consisting of all the positions a point can have according to a certain rule

lower quartile   the value that divides a set of data into a lower quarter and an upper three-quarters

lowest common multiple   the lowest number that each of two or more numbers will divide exactly into, e.g. LCM of 14 and 16 is 112

mean   sum of all the values ÷ number of values

median   the middle value when data is arranged in order

mode	the value that occurs most often
moving average	a 3-point moving average is the mean of each 3 successive values in a data set
multiple	an integer into which a smaller integer divides exactly
numerator	the top number in a fraction
per cent	number of parts per hundred
perimeter	distance all round a shape
plan	view of an object from directly above
power	8 is 2 to the power 3; three 2s multiplied together make 8
prime number	an integer with only two factors: itself and 1
quadratic	expression or equation with an x^2 term
range	difference between highest and lowest values in a set of data
ratio	two numbers expressing the relative sizes of two quantities
reciprocal	a number multiplied by its reciprocal is equal to 1
recurring decimal	a number in which a pattern of digits repeats endlessly after the decimal point
reflection	the image of an object in a mirror line
reflection symmetry	a line or plane of symmetry divides a shape into matching halves

rotation	the turning of an object about a point
rotation symmetry	the order of rotational symmetry is the number of identical positions a shape has in one revolution
sequence	a set of numbers with a pattern
similar	the same shape but not the same size
simplify	collect like terms; cancel fractions
simultaneous equations	two equations with x and y terms; their solution is the point where their graphs cross
square root	the number which, when multiplied by itself, is equal to the given number
standard index form	a number expressed as a number between 1 and 10 multiplied by a power of 10
surd	square root of a prime number or of of a multiple of a prime number
tangent	a line that touches a curve
translation	moving an object in a straight line
upper quartile	the value that divides a set of data into an upper quarter and a lower three-quarters

Useful Websites

Here are some websites which may help with your exam preparations.

www.schoolshistory.org.uk/maths.htm

www.bbc.co.uk/schools/gcsebitesize/maths

www.gcse.com/maths/pre.htm

www.mathslessons.co.uk

www.easymaths.com

www.learn.co.uk

www.gcsemaths.fsnet.co.uk

www.maths-help.co.uk

www.projectgcse.co.uk/maths

www.s-cool.co.uk

www.easymaths.com

www.letts-education.com

Index

First published in Great Britain in 2002 by Virgin Books Ltd and Letts Educational Ltd

Virgin Books Ltd
Thames Wharf Studios
Rainville Road
London
W6 9HA

Letts Educational Ltd
Chiswick Centre
414 Chiswick High Road
London
W4 5TF

Copyright © 2002 Virgin Books Ltd/Letts Educational Ltd
Design and Illustration © 2002 Virgin Books Ltd/Letts Educational Ltd

A catalogue record for this book is available from the British Library.

ISBN 0 7535 0663 7

Prepared by *specialist* publishing services, Milton Keynes
Printed and bound in Great Britain by Clays, Suffolk

Letts Educational Ltd is a division of Granada Learning Ltd, part of the Granada Group.